LIVING HOMES FOR CULTURAL EXPRESSION

NMAI EDITIONS

LIVING HOMES
FOR CULTURAL EXPRESSION

North American Native Perspectives on Creating Community Museums

KAREN COODY COOPER & NICOLASA I. SANDOVAL
Editors

National Museum of the American Indian
Smithsonian Institution
Washington, D.C., and New York
2006

Library of Congress Cataloging-in-Publication Data

Living homes for cultural expression : North American Native perspectives on creating community museums / Karen Coody Cooper and Nicolasa I. Sandoval, editors.
    p. cm.

ISBN 0-9719163-8-1 (alk. paper)
1. Indians of North America—Museums. 2. Indian arts—United States. 3. Ethnological museums and collections—United States. 4. Minority arts facilities—United States. 5. Community centers—United States. 6. Community development—United States. I. Cooper, Karen Coody. II. Sandoval, Nicolasa I. III. National Museum of the American Indian (U.S.)

E56.L58 2005
305.897'0075—dc22
2005016415

Manufactured in the United States of America
The paper used in this publication meets the minimum requirements of the American National Standard for Permanence of Paper for Printed Library Materials 239.48-1984.

National Museum of the American Indian
Project Director: Terence Winch, Head of Publications
Editors: Tanya Thrasher, Amy Pickworth, Duncan Primeaux, and Kate Mitchell
Designer: Steve Bell

The Smithsonian's National Museum of the American Indian works in collaboration with the Native peoples of the Western Hemisphere and Hawai'i to protect and foster indigenous cultures, reaffirm traditions and beliefs, encourage contemporary artistic expression, and provide a forum for Native voices. Through its publishing program, NMAI's Publications Office seeks to augment awareness of Native American beliefs and lifeways and to educate the public about the history and significance of Native cultures. NMAI's Community Services Department is a cornerstone of the museum's commitment to outreach, providing a vital link between our staff and collections and Native communities.

For information about the Smithsonian's National Museum of the American Indian, visit the NMAI website at www.AmericanIndian.si.edu. To support the museum by becoming a member, call 1-800-242-NMAI (6624) or click on "Support" on our website.

Title Page: Roberta Kirk (Warm Springs) and Irvine Scalplock (Siksika Nation) examine a basket during a 1996 training workshop at the Museum at Warm Springs, Oregon. Photograph by Karen Coody Cooper.

TABLE OF CONTENTS

NICOLASA I. SANDOVAL

FOREWORD

THIS ASSEMBLY OF STORIES—from an Alutiiq community on Alaska's Kodiak Island to Hopi people in Arizona—speaks to the concerns and aspirations that unite indigenous peoples in the lands known now as the Americas. The wealth of knowledge brimming from these accounts informs and inspires those who have chosen a journey of great challenges and greater rewards—that of creating a tribal museum. The path of life knows no finite borders or clear maps. There are only moments in time throughout the journey where we find safe places to be who we are and to define ourselves in our own terms. The National Museum of the American Indian (NMAI) continues to play a vital role as both a haven and hub for many beautifully radiant forms of expression. The hemispheric scope of perspectives presented at the NMAI affirms its commitment to education and public service, which transcends boundaries and narrows distances between people.

Community-based museums and cultural centers strengthen the bonds that connect generations. We remember ourselves in these places and dream about who we want to be. At their best, these places are homes for cultural expression, dialogue, learning, and understanding. They serve the communities and people who initiated them, as well as wider audiences, by stimulating cultural activism and continuity that endures for the sake of all our children. While listening to stories of individuals who have assumed significant roles in the development of a museum or cultural center, we may recognize the familiar. In her piece on volunteerism and its role in maintaining museums, Marilyn C. Hudson recalls the generosity of Helen Gough, an Arikara member of the Three Affiliated Tribes, whose bequest initiated a heritage center for the Mandan, Hidatsa, and Arikara people more than forty years ago. As in many other communities, the essence of giving and commitment to subsequent generations continues to light our path.

The voices in this compendium speak of the celebration and struggle that emerge from sustaining and expanding community-based museums and cultural centers. In her description of public programs development at the Alutiiq Museum, Amy F. Steffian recounts the deliberate, but difficult, choice to invite external partnership. Given the systemic wresting of cultures, languages, and lives from Native peoples that followed for centuries after Contact, it is understood that, for indigenous people, decisions to include agencies and institutions as collaborators do not come without careful consideration and willingness to believe that a new history may begin to unfold. Community-based museums and cultural centers are places where we may bear witness to this transformation.

The spirit of generosity unfolds in these pages. Each of the writers freely shares the wealth of his or her unique experiences. They are the mothers and fathers who have borne and nurtured these places known as tribal museums, raising them for the benefit of their respective communities and for all of us who are invited to learn the wisdom imbued in their stories.

KAREN COODY COOPER

PREFACE

IF TWO WORDS WERE TO DESCRIBE THE MISSION of the National Museum of the American Indian, they would be "cultural continuance." What makes our efforts unique throughout mainstream museum work is that our exhibitions and programs are grounded in the authority of the Native perspective. Part of our ongoing outreach efforts—and the one that we hope this book will address—is assisting Native communities as they interpret, collect, and care for their own collections, thereby making Native voices heard by the museum community at large.

There are about 200 Native community museums in Canada, Mexico, and the United States. It is important to note that the terms "Native community museum" or "tribal museum" used in this book do not simply refer to museums with a collection of Native American materials. We have looked, rather, to the type of authority that governs these museums as a way to more accurately define them. Museums that retain Native authority through direct tribal ownership or majority presence, or that are located on tribally controlled lands, or that have a Native director or board members are the institutions that meet our criteria.

Tribal museums are a relatively new museum category. Three tribal museums were founded before 1940, and two more opened in the decade that followed. In the 1950s, six opened; in the 1960s, fifteen; and in the 1970s, the forty-five that opened more than doubled the total number of Native-managed museums in the Western Hemisphere. In the 1980s, another thirty-

Karen Coody Cooper (front row, second from right) and NMAI curator Emil Her Many Horses (far left) with Sicangu Heritage Center staff on the Rosebud Sioux Reservation in Mission, South Dakota. Photograph by Jill Norwood.

five museums opened, and the 1990s saw at least forty more. In the coming years, hundreds of new community-based museums could potentially open their doors.

Eager to tell their stories, Native communities are no longer entrusting non-Native institutions to define who they are. As a result, Native community museums have encouraged self-awareness within the larger museum field—evaluating relations with their respective audiences as well as reconsidering their conditioned approach to handling material culture. In fact, many tribal cultural institutions refuse to use the term "museum," reinforcing the message that for some Native people the word carries negative connotations and strong associations with the egregious treatment Native communities received (and, in some instances, still receive) at the hands of museums.

We anticipate that this book marks the beginning of a long-term collaboration between the National Museum of the American Indian and Native communities. If you wish to contribute comments or additional information about this important topic, please contact me at cooperk@si.edu.

Albuquerque's Indian Pueblo Cultural Center represents nineteen Pueblo tribes of New Mexico with museum, performance, and meeting spaces; sales outlets; and a restaurant. Photograph by Karen Coody Cooper.

KAREN COODY COOPER

Starting a Native Museum or Cultural Center

SOME NATIVE COMMUNITIES ASPIRE TO START THEIR OWN MUSEUMS or cultural centers, or to refocus their existing facilities. Some communities want to attract tourists. Other communities primarily want a place to preserve and present their history and culture to their own community. And some want to serve both audiences. This essay has been divided into key elements to consider if you are building a center for your community, and issues of importance to those focused on creating a center to attract outside public.

The first step in developing a cultural center or museum should be canvassing members of your community to see what they prefer and what priorities exist. Is there enough interest to support a museum effort? Should the museum be for tourists or strictly for community use? For instance, does your community want to encourage the continuation of traditional arts through sales (tourists might be good), or is language preservation a priority (a community center might be best)? Listen to people's concerns. Consider how those concerns might best be met. Select a cause in which you can succeed. One success can then lead to another.

Starting a Community Museum or Cultural Center

- Call a meeting of local people interested in the project and find out in what ways they are willing to help and what their interests and abilities are. Then use their volunteer efforts as you continue. Encourage them to tap into personal connections they might have with talented or influential people.

- Keep the community informed about your progress through mailings, posted bulletins, radio, newspapers/newsletters, meetings, and events. Developing an annual event is one way to start the project before you have a home for it and to garner attention, as well as a means of tracking progress.

- Ascertain the practical scope of the project. Should it be kept small and grow gradually, or should you plan big and seek extensive external funding? "Small" means "grass roots," and can often serve community needs responsibly without overburdening community resources. A large facility is expensive to build and maintain and may not seem welcoming to many in the community.

- Develop a planning process. Don't be too rigid or too lax. Take time to plan the use of space carefully. A museum/center usually requires space for a lobby or entrance; exhibitions and hands-on activities; rooms for receiving and storing collections, public and staff meetings, and lectures and crafts demonstrations; a museum store (and more storage); bathrooms, kitchenette, and adequate offices for staff (and storage for office and building supplies); and a support library and archives. Is there a building locally that can be used, or is a new building required?

- Decide how governance will be organized. Will your community government control the museum, or will it be controlled by an independent board of interested individuals, probably from the community, plus experts from outside? Who will pay the salaries of employees? Occasionally hybrid situations arise, such as a government budget paying for a core number of employees while an independent board sees to the management of the museum with a director it selects.

- Visit existing museums and cultural centers to learn what you need to know about the field. Make appointments to speak to curators, educators, and directors. Learn about museum organizations, museum literature, and museum policies and practices.

- Obtain sample museum/cultural center policies and forms. Build up a small reference library of museum literature.

- Develop your policies and plans and formally organize your group. Establish a budget and begin fundraising. You're on your way!

Starting a Tourist Museum

- Consider whether tourists can and will come. Is there highway access? Are you on the way to successful tourist sites? Are there gas stations, restaurants, and hotels nearby? Is there too much competition or none at all? If none at all, will you provide enough activities to warrant an excursion to your museum?

- Consider what an influx of tourists might be like in your community. Will they be welcomed? The museum might best be located outside the community on a busy highway, in a larger neighboring community, or by a historical or natural site of interest. If located in your community, consider how best to protect the privacy of homes in the area, control litter, and address issues of parking, erosion, etc.

- Consider the resources at your disposal. A successful tourist museum requires well-designed brochures, advertisements, a website, and publicity to compete with other activities. Exhibits must be professional and attractive. Operating hours must be extensive, especially on weekends. Amenities such as food and beverages might be required, especially if your location is isolated. Staffing needs to be adequate for service, safety, and security.

- Develop realistic economic expectations. Tourism can generate income, but it is affected by outside factors such as gasoline prices, economic turns, and how safe or practical people feel it is to travel. Contingency funds need to be in place to carry you through low visitation periods.

- Make it easy to find your museum. Arrange for highway signs, and put up a good sign on your own property. Develop an easy-to-read map for your brochures, and put it on your website as well.

- Make sure your building has adequate space for busloads of people. Receptions, parties, and events might also be held there. Such a building, when air-conditioned, usually requires entrance doors that provide an air-lock, meaning two sets of doors before the entrance to the lobby. A loading dock will be needed for traveling exhibits and borrowed collections. Security systems are recommended. Roadways and parking must be in good condition. Outdoor lighting and picnic facilities should be considered. Bathrooms must accommodate large numbers of visitors.

- Start attending national or regional museum association annual meetings and enrolling in museum staff development workshops. Obtain copies of museum job descriptions in preparation for hiring additional people.

- Be prepared for large-scale planning. Funding will usually need to come from many sources. Proposals will need to be well-written, and planning documents will need to be polished. If you don't hire a fundraiser, your committee will need to request examples of successful proposals from funding sources and from other similar projects to begin gathering and compiling your proposal information.

Every community and every museum is unique. There is no exact formula to follow because there is no other community exactly like yours. Additionally, things change through time. What worked a decade ago may not work now. Laws and practices change. Once you have opened your museum, remember that change is inevitable. Don't expect to operate the same way ten years from now. Constantly assess and prepare for the future, and remember that your museum is helping to shape the future as well.

RESOURCES

Erikson, Patricia Pierce. *Voices of a Thousand People: The Makah Cultural and Research Center.* Lincoln: University of Nebraska Press, 2002.

Guyette, Susan. *Planning for Balanced Development: A Guide for Native American and Rural Communities.* Santa Fe: Clear Light Publishers, 1996.

Stapp, Darby C., and Michael S. Burney. *Tribal Cultural Resource Management: The Full Circle to Stewardship.* Lanham, MD: AltaMira Press, 2002.

Also refer to the museum book catalogs of the American Association of Museums (AAM) and the American Association for State and Local History (AASLH).

Rick Hill guiding museum interpreters in the *Pathways of Tradition* exhibition at the NMAI's George Gustav Heye Center, New York, 1992. Photograph by NMAI Photo Services staff.

RICHARD W. HILL SR.

Road Map for Native Museum Exhibition Planning

If you only had thirty minutes to tell someone about the most important aspects of your community—its culture and arts, its history, and its people—what would you say? That is the dilemma you create for yourself when you decide to build a museum, visitor center, or cultural center. The real challenge behind exhibition planning is to tell "stories" through which visitors can imagine what others' lives are like.

As a form of storytelling, an exhibition is a communicative act that must be animated and memorable, just like the storytelling of the past. The stories you decide to tell, however, will most likely differ from the ones you would tell if time permitted. It's best to consider strategies for more effective narrative and visitor experience.

First: You will have very little time. Most visitors will not spend more than one hour at your museum. People get tired walking around in museum spaces. They generally become disoriented in museums that are large, dark boxes with bright lights that are hard on the eyes. Finding ways to make the visit more exciting will encourage people to stay and explore more of your stories.

Second: People don't like to read a lot in museums. Often, too much time is spent writing labels, only to find that people might look at a display case for fewer than thirty seconds. Visitors will seek out a label only if something really interests them. Too much text disrupts the mood.

Third: Stereotypes about Indians and other indigenous peoples invade the thinking of even the most enlightened museum visitor. Visitors have pre-conceived ideas that they want verified by your museum. You have to under-stand your audience if you want to educate them.

Fourth: The needs of the community and the needs of the visiting pub-lic are different. A good museum provides a substantial museum experience for both audiences. It needs to be a place of learning for all.

This essay provides you with a practical step-by-step approach to con-ceptualizing, planning, and designing museum exhibitions. It cannot answer all of the questions you might have, but it will give you a road map to use as you make your own way along the journey. There are no standards that will apply to all communities or all facilities. You must decide for yourself what works best.

As a member of the Mall Exhibitions Master Planning Team for the Na-tional Museum of the American Indian, I had the opportunity to visit mu-seums, large and small, across North America. To summarize what I learned about exhibition planning, the main areas of concern are as follows:

• The exhibits are more than objects in display cases. The most effective exhibitions create an atmosphere for learning and immerse the visitor in the cultural environment of the community. The visit to the museum should be a multisensory experience that stimulates a sense of awe and wonder, so that visitors will want to learn more.

• Exhibits that work best take into account human nature and different styles of learning. Visitors must discover their own way to move through the museum. People need to connect to the story on a very human level, to find something of themselves in the exhibition. In this way, it will be easier for them to identify with themes, topics, and subjects of the exhi-bition, and they will remember more clearly what they learned.

• Exhibit planning takes time, and many points of view must be consid-ered at first. The process involves selecting and editing the stories to be told from the totality of material collected.

- Exhibition plans undergo great transformations as they develop. What you end up with might be very different from what you envisioned in the beginning.

I) Steps for Exhibition Development

These are some common steps that most museums take in planning their exhibitions. You might have to adjust them to your unique situation.

- Examine the **mission statement** of your organization.

- Develop clear **goals** for the project that support the mission statement.

- Identify the **topics** for the exhibition and why they are important.

- Identify the **themes** tying those topics together that you want to share with the public.

- Identify the underlying **cultural values, beliefs, and ethics** that not only drive those themes but also explain their importance.

- Research and collect **Native oral histories and literature** on the topics, and develop background papers on each topic.

- Locate potential **objects** relating to the themes and cultural processes that might be used to illustrate the story.

- Locate potential **photographs** illustrating the topics and places of focus in the exhibition.

- Create a **flow chart** of how the topics link together, identifying the main sections of the exhibition, the educational objective(s) of each section, the Native themes of each section, and the subthemes to be presented.

- Explore various ways of presenting the story and determine the **style of interpretation** that will be most effective for each section of the exhibition.

- Write the **preliminary script**, which outlines the exhibition, briefly stating the main information, its Native perspective, and the focus of each section of the exhibition.

- Solicit **review** of and comments on the script from advisors, and make the appropriate adjustments.

- Write the **final script,** including main text panel, sub-text panels, object labels, object list, photo list, and photo captions. It may take several drafts and rewrites of the script before it meets with everyone's approval.

There may be many variations on these tasks. Every museum will have a different mix of ideas based on their particular experience. Gerard Hilferty & Associates applied a team strategy to the National Museum of the American Indian that generated the following steps in exhibition planning:

- Interpretive Goals and Objectives

- Interpretive Approach

- Catalog of Exhibition Themes

- Approach for Use of Collections

- Educational Strategies

- Interpretive Media Concepts

- Statement of Principal Exhibition Messages

II) Who Is Going To Tell This Story?
Selecting the Exhibition Development Team

Creating a good exhibition is a team effort. Team building becomes one of the first steps to give knowledgeable individuals the authority to make decisions in the exhibition development process. The exhibition team should be comprised of staff, a few board members, and contracted consultants to identify the themes that will be selected for the interpretive programs. The team needs to develop its own frame of reference with a concise mission statement, so that everyone understands what they are trying to accomplish, who is responsible for what tasks, and when the results are expected. The team should not be more than five people, as getting more people to come together and reach agreements at each step along the way becomes cumbersome.

An exhibition team leader should be appointed to work with the primary staff/contracted specialist to assure that the project continues in a timely manner. The exhibition team leader is also responsible for assuring that the work of the team is reflective of the mission of the team and the project, and coordinates with the other aspects of the museum or cultural center.

The exhibition team needs to orient itself to its tasks and available resources and develop its own way of getting business done. Members should meet monthly to select exhibition themes, explore the cultural concepts behind the themes, determine case-work subjects, and identify potential objects; they should also supervise the development of the primary storyline for all of the interpretive components of the museum or cultural center. Every time the team meets, their development plans must show all of the milestones to be accomplished, from the conceptual stage to the opening date of the facility.

What should the team consider?

It might be helpful to share with the exhibition team some of the current thinking on why people visit museums in the first place. The team should study any related visitor studies, planning documents, local curriculum, and market research, if it exists. It is a good idea to develop a reference list for each team member to read, both on the process and on the subject matter of the exhibitions. In a 1990 report, "Unity of All Creation—A New Paradigm for the National Museum of Natural History," that museum's director for public programs, Robert Sullivan, outlined some beliefs about museum visitors:

• First and foremost, **visitors are living individuals** and not abstract demographic statistics.

- Visitors should feel **expected, welcomed, and comfortable**, and the museum, as a good host, first takes care of their basic needs for orientation, seats, bathrooms, and occasional quiet.

- Visitor **questions should be anticipated and honored**, beyond what the museum feels is important.

- Visitors **should not feel diminished, ignorant, foolish, powerless, or excluded.**

- Visitors should feel that the museum is **responsive and interactive**.

- The museum should strive to **reach each visitor**, and regard each **individual as unique.**

The Strong Museum in Rochester, New York, posted its philosophy about how children learn best in museums. These are good ideas that can help you develop your own philosophy about how your museum will inform, enlighten, and inspire visitors. Children learn:

- When they **explore** at their own pace;

- When they **discover** by their own means;

- When they make their own **decisions;**

- When they are using all their **senses;**

- When they are **listening to and telling stories;**

- When they are **playing with words;**

- When they are **playing and learning with parents.**

The exhibition team must also consider how the museum exhibition fits into the overall educational strategy of the community. What is already being taught? How well is it working? What needs to be improved?

All too often the Native museum is thought of primarily as a tourist facility within an economic development plan. While cultural tourism is important to consider, your exhibitions must have credibility with your own
people if they are to be successful. Your exhibitions should be an extension
of the cultural values of the community.

III) Conceptual Development of the Story

There are no surefire ways to determine themes for exhibition. This process,
however, will help you identify the possibilities and weed out what might
not work. Some themes are too complex or require too much background
knowledge, while others are too sacred to work very well in an exhibition.
In any case, the team will have to develop a list of themes by whatever process
works best for them. Once those themes are selected and approved by the
powers that be, the team can then proceed with the basic steps in the process:

- **Research on the subject matter**: What are the specific topics to be
  discussed?

- **Interpretation of the museum mission statement**: How will these topics reflect the overarching goals of the museum?

- **Interpretive concept development**: How a report on the findings of the
  team may include the following:

    Interpretive goals and objectives
    Overall interpretive approach
    Educational strategies
    Statement of principal exhibition messages

- **Exhibition concept development**: This is the development and writing
  of story outlines and relationship diagrams. These will identify the major
  themes, subthemes, topics, and messages of the exhibition, and relation-
  ships between the stories.

- **Script development:** Each script outline would then be reviewed and refined on the way to producing a preliminary exhibition script.

What are the ideas about your community that you want visitors to better understand?

It is important for the exhibition team you assemble to assure that Native perspectives are well-represented in the planning. Those involved should always remember that a successful plan considers the following:

- The museum should provide a **clear orientation** for visitors.

- Visitors should be made to **feel welcomed** and comfortable.

- Exhibition cases, labels, and audio-visual presentations should be **easy to see and understand**.

- The ideas behind the exhibition need to be **sequenced** so that the totality of the museum experience is recalled.

- Spaces must be **accessible** to persons with exceptional physical need or to large school groups.

- Designs must be **flexible** to adjust to changes in scholarship, objects, or visitor responsiveness.

- Programs and exhibitions need to be **evaluated regularly** to make sure that visitors are learning and enjoying their visits.

- The museum has **multiple audiences**—the local community, Native visitors, tourists, schools, etc. Programs must be designed to reach each of these distinct audiences, and visitor research is an important way to measure the effectiveness in satisfying their diverse interests.

- The staff should be prepared to change what is not working and change it fast. The museum **must be current**.

Participants in a training workshop at the Tunica-Biloxi Museum in Marksville, Louisiana, examine insect damage to baskets from their respective museum collections. The Tunica-Biloxi Museum was established when the tribe gained possession of artifacts that had been pillaged from an ancestral site. Photograph by Karen Coody Cooper.

Establishing a concise statement of philosophy and mission of the museum or cultural center is an important first step in helping shape the story. The project needs a Native attitude to guide the overall thinking. A clear, unified statement in the beginning will make it easier to answer unforeseen questions about topics ranging from Native foods to toys to canoes.

The Alutiiq Center in downtown Kodiak. The Alutiiq Museum occupies the first floor of the two-story building in the center of the photograph. Photograph © Sven Haakanson, Jr.

AMY F. STEFFIAN

Teaching Traditions: Public Programming at the Alutiiq Museum

I believe that when Native communities involve others in learning and promoting their history, the results are extremely positive. Not only do we succeed in meeting our own objectives, uplifting Native youth for example, but we tear down stereotypes, create greater opportunity, and build a more accepting world. . . . We can preserve what is dear to us by sharing it, by making it valuable to everyone. . . . It is not enough for the Alutiiq to know ourselves—everyone must know us. [1]

—Ruth A. Dawson
Chair, Alutiiq Heritage Foundation, 2003

OUT OF THE DARK AND DRIZZLE THAT MARK SPRINGTIME around Kodiak Island, Alaska, students tread into a tiny rural school in Ouzinkie, a village of no more than 170, located on the southwest shore of Spruce Island. For schools like this one, all is brightened during Alutiiq Week—an annual, island-wide celebration of Alutiiq heritage held in area schools. One of the eight major groups of Alaska Natives, the Alutiiq people have inhabited the expansive, ecologically varied coast of central Alaska for millennia. During Alutiiq Week, students of all ages study traditional songs and dances, explore Native arts, practice the Alutiiq language, and prepare traditional foods.

Among the participants in Ouzinkie Alutiiq Week 2002 were carvers from the Alutiiq Museum, a Native-governed culture center and storage facility in the nearby city of Kodiak. The artists arrived by a chartered twin-engine plane with three peculiar wooden crates. In the school lobby, the crates were opened to reveal an exhibit on Alutiiq masks, part of the museum's Carving Traditions workshop. Displays of raw materials, carving tools, and prehistoric artifacts were designed to provide inspiration for students as they explore Alutiiq culture through woodworking—an art once essential to daily life.

Students pored over pictures of ancestral masks, studied replicas of prehistoric tools, plotted dimensions in pencil for their own carvings, and then created masks. The artists leading the workshop taught classical forms and finishes, and encouraged students to combine traditional elements with original designs. Parents and elders joined the carving sessions, strengthening intergenerational ties through heritage exploration. At the end of the workshop, students had the opportunity to lend their creations to the Alutiiq Museum for display in Kodiak, and to view their work on the museum's website alongside examples of student carvings from four other villages.[2]

This classroom scene may seem unremarkable, but it reflects a dramatic change in the way Kodiak children learn about history. The Alutiiq people are one of Alaska's least-known Native groups. The conquest of Kodiak by Russian fur traders led to an early and profoundly disruptive period of cultural change. The catastrophic loss of life, combined with the loss of political sovereignty and economic self-sufficiency, suppressed the transmission of cultural traditions. Nearly erased, Alutiiq culture survived in fragments that were rarely shared. This has been particularly evident in Kodiak's classrooms. Until recently, school curricula focused on the two centuries of Alaska's Russian and American history, excluding nearly eight millennia of the Alutiiq past. Today, however, museum-led collaborations for heritage education, like Carving Traditions, are reawakening traditions and restoring Native history to community consciousness.

Carving Traditions was one of a series of workshops in the museum's Traveling Traditions program, produced annually in partnership with the

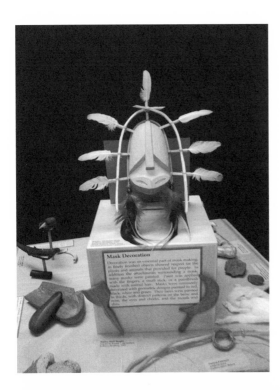

Left and below: Carving Traditions displays of Alutiiq masks. Photographs © Sven Haakanson, Jr.

Ouzinkie students and teachers study photographs of Alutiiq masks.
Photograph © Sven Haakanson, Jr.

Kodiak Island Borough School District. Created with grants from Native corporations, private foundations, and public agencies, the Traveling Traditions program meets multiple goals. At the general level, the program preserves and shares Alutiiq heritage by spreading knowledge of time-honored arts—carving, weaving, and skin sewing. At a deeper level, it promotes respect. In collaboration with the school district, Traveling Traditions reaches underserved audiences outside the museum gallery. This partnership also provides an opportunity for educators—who are not always sympathetic to the need for cultural education—to explore Alutiiq traditions. As with all of its programs, the museum designed Traveling Traditions to elevate perceptions of Native people and instill a sense of dignity in Native youth.

Practically speaking, programs like Traveling Traditions are not difficult to develop. Researching traditions, assembling displays, working with artists, and teaching students are activities that museums perform frequently and well. The real hurdle is to reach beyond museum walls—that is, beyond the organization's immediate group of supporters—to create an experience with broad, lasting impact. Traveling Traditions continues to succeed because of the museum's partnership with the Kodiak school district. Had the program been hosted in the museum gallery or without the involvement of teachers, its impact would have been very different. The collaborative approach underlying Traveling Traditions reflects both the evolution of the museum and a philosophy that emerged as the organization struggled to define itself and secure a meaningful place in the Kodiak community.

Akhiok student J. R. Amodo with a mask completed in the 2001 Carving Traditions workshop. Photograph © Sven Haakanson, Jr.

Programs Create the Museum

The Alutiiq Museum's story begins in the late 1970s, when the leadership of the Kodiak Area Native Association (KANA)[3]—a nonprofit organization that provides healthcare and social services to Kodiak's Native people—recognized the reawakening and preserving of Alutiiq traditions as essential to community healing.

In 1984 an opportunity for heritage revival came when Gordon Pullar, president of KANA, agreed to fund a modest excavation led by the late archaeologist Dr. Richard Jordan. In return for KANA's support, researchers would involve youth in excavations planned in the village of Karluk and share their finds at a day-long community celebration. The Karluk Archaeological Project unearthed a water-saturated, remarkably preserved winter settlement with rare wooden artifacts—carved bowls, harpoons, fish spears, armor, amulets, and masks. At the end of the season, people from across the archipelago flew to Karluk to tour the site, see the finds, and share in a potlatch (a celebratory feast). Here, emotion shifted from anger to bewilderment among Alutiiqs, who had believed their forebearers to be impoverished stone tool users rather than the skilled artisans who produced the treasures presented in the community gymnasium.[4]

After several seasons of additional research, KANA hired archaeologist Rick Knecht to develop cultural programming and establish a museum. There were no facilities. Knecht didn't even have a desk. He sat in a hallway at KANA and wrote his first grant proposal on a clipboard. Community interest was solid, however, and a suite of programs developed rapidly. Programs included kayak and sod-house building (a traditional Alutiiq house built partially underground); projects in language, oral history, and dance; and arts workshops and symposia.[5]

Led mostly by KANA staff, these projects focused on outreach to the Alutiiq community, but gradually attracted a larger audience and began to involve community partners. One major obstacle remained. There was no place to store collections. The Karluk artifacts, the objects that had ignited the heritage movement, were stored in a distant university. With cultural programs blossoming, KANA initiated plans for a museum.

The tragic Exxon *Valdez* oil spill, which strewed crude oil across the Alutiiq homeland in the summer of 1989, provided the opportunity to build the museum. With its educational programs underway and community interest in heritage education broadening, KANA leaders argued that restoration dollars should be spent to create a museum for the Native community. Their compelling argument resulted in a $1.5 million grant to build a cultural center and storage facility—the Alutiiq Museum and Archaeological Repository—to be governed by representatives of eight Alutiiq organizations. KANA was able to fund construction because the museum's heart—its heritage programs—was already beating.

A Challenging Start

The new museum presented a mountain of challenges. For the first time since the days of chiefs, shamans, and religious specialists, the Alutiiq had a central source of cultural information, and many began a joyous exploration of their heritage. The museum's potential wasn't lost on the teachers, researchers, land managers, and tour operators who swarmed the facility. But meeting the demand for access to cultural information proved as daunting as funding and staffing the facility.

The museum's board of directors quickly recognized that it had neither the resources nor the staff to meet this overwhelming demand for services. The museum could limp forward, responding to other organizations' needs, or develop its own programs in partnership with the Kodiak community, with which it would share project costs and workloads while educating audiences beyond museum walls. To reach these audiences, the museum would take its ideas to organizations that might help: schools, social service providers, and the media.

To an Alutiiq community that had a painful history of interaction with Western educational institutions, government agencies, and the like, the museum's choice to partner with non-Native organizations was not always popular. Alutiiqs had struggled for two centuries to regain control of the institutions that governed their societies. Why then should "others" be invited to partner in heritage education, a process at the heart of perpetuating Alutiiq culture? The question surfaced early in the museum's history. Some museum leaders felt heritage education should be run by and for Natives. Others saw an opportunity to better serve Alutiiqs by involving a larger community, following the example of KANA's archaeological projects. These differences in opinion among Native leaders intensified until the museum found itself in a dilemma.

A Philosophy for Programming

After a number of administrative problems—including the inability to find and keep a director, financial insecurity, and the failure of a gift shop—the museum's governing organizations began to lose faith in the facility's viability. Moreover, supporters questioned whether museum programs were really reaching the Alutiiq community. Were community partnerships really in the best interest of Alutiiq people or were they simply serving others? To keep the organization on track, the board of directors responded with long-range planning. Over three months, the board and staff met periodically to document their collective vision. Though they designed no programs, the group established a clear philosophy for programming—one whose tenets could be realistically met.

An "Alutiiq first" philosophy followed. As a Native Alaskan-governed organization, the Alutiiq Museum would serve the Alutiiq people first. Museum programs would promote knowledge of Alutiiq culture and history to reawaken traditions and strengthen pride in Native people. This focus would be paired with education of the entire Kodiak community to elevate perceptions of Native people. The museum would wear down cultural stereotypes by inviting everyone to participate in preserving, sharing, and learning about Alutiiq heritage.

This approach had immediate benefits. First, the museum's governing organizations saw the links between the museum's mission and its programs more clearly. No longer suspect, community collaboration became a source of pride and reason for support. Second, the museum improved its teamwork. With a shared set of goals, the board and the staff had a unified message. This brought in grant money, helped to justify expenses, and ultimately led to the development of more partnerships and successful programs.

Lessons in Programming

In developing public programs, the museum faced a number of difficulties. After the excitement of the museum's opening, it became a challenge to attract gallery visitors. First, it was difficult to serve the geographically dispersed Alutiiq community. Although the museum is located in the city of Kodiak, fewer than one thousand of the three thousand people represented by the museum's governing organizations live in this regional population center. The rest reside in six wilderness villages accessible only by boat or plane. Others have moved to the city of Anchorage and beyond. Thus, many Alutiiqs could not visit the museum or participate in traditional types of programs.

Similarly, while Kodiak residents flooded the museum in its first months, many never returned. Visitors perceived that they could learn everything in one museum visit. Others wondered what a Native museum could offer people of other heritages. How could museum programming include a wider audience if people couldn't or wouldn't visit the museum?

The first lesson the staff learned was that the community's existing channels of communication—classrooms, events, the media, and the Internet—could connect the Native community with the museum and thereby develop a larger audience at home and afar. The museum would have to be the starting place for cultural education, not the final stop.

With educators repeatedly requesting assistance in developing lessons on Alutiiq culture, the museum created traveling educational boxes for use in elementary school classrooms. Each box had its own theme and set of activities and curriculum ideas. There was no charge to check out the boxes, which were packaged for easy shipping. The boxes were a huge success. Within a year, they visited every school in the archipelago and Alaskan mainland and even schools in other states.

Another early program took advantage of an existing resource—the artwork produced in rural schools. The exploration of Alaska Native crafts not only had educational value, it promoted self-expression. Recognizing the growing awareness of Native heritage among children by their newfound pride in traditional arts, the museum invited the Kodiak Island Borough School District to gather exemplary student artwork for a spring exhibit.

The debut of the Rural School Art Show drew thirty-six works from seven schools.

The museum exhibited the art during the annual school trips to Kodiak. This meant that village students were able to see their art professionally displayed and view the work of their peers. For those who couldn't travel to Kodiak, the museum created a photo album of the show that traveled to each community. Local tradition bearers and artists volunteered to judge the show and retailers donated art supplies for prizes. This program was a great way to begin connecting with rural audiences. It linked both individuals and schools with the museum, creating positive ties. And collaboration with the school district kept the costs minimal.

A more ambitious program developed in partnership with the media. In isolated Kodiak, the museum befriended members of the media by consistently sharing museum news and responding reliably to requests for information. Media coverage of museum news captivated the community. As the *Alutiiq Word of the Week* radio series would reveal, KMXT Public Radio and tribal culture were a good fit.

The *Alutiiq Word of the Week* began as a two-minute radio spot that paired Alutiiq vocabulary with a short cultural lesson. To make the lessons relevant to life around Kodiak, each lesson matched the season. Lessons on boating and fishing aired during the summer, while those on gift-giving and feasting aired over the winter holidays. Copies of the lessons were posted at the museum and filed in a gallery notebook. Requests for lesson copies increased. People were posting them at work, sticking them to the fridge, and keeping them in notebooks. To meet the demand, the museum established fax and email broadcast systems to transmit the lessons inexpensively. The *Kodiak Daily Mirror* published the feature as a column in its Friday edition. In a matter of weeks, this simple but informative program reached over 14,000 people, bringing Alutiiq traditions to most households in the Kodiak archipelago.

The popularity of *Alutiiq Word of the Week* stressed the need for accurate sources of cultural information written for a general audience. Thus, staff used the most frequently asked visitor questions to develop a series of free, nicely formatted educational handouts that could be picked up in the gallery, mailed and e-mailed to patrons, and packaged with museum store merchandise. Each purchase of jewelry adorned with petroglyph images, for example, came with a handout on Alutiiq rock art. Like the *Alutiiq Word of the Week* lessons, the handouts were popular, though expensive to stock.

Eventually, the demand for educational materials, motivated by the ongoing effort to serve communities beyond the museum, led to the development of a museum website. Posted were educational handouts and electronic versions of *Alutiiq Word of the Week* and the Rural School Art Show, as well as advertisements for events and store merchandise. The website remains an integral part of museum programs. Temporary web pages for each major program provide access to its resources. By 2002, the site had received more than 35,000 hits. As the electronic guestbook suggests, the website allows Alutiiq people from all over the world to keep in touch with their heritage.

What a joy and delight to know that there are others like me in the world. For someone who is not close geographically to the land of her ancestors, I truly enjoy how this "super-information highway" can bring me closer to what is my heritage (if not physically, then spiritually. . . . It will be through this site that I will be able to become more knowledgeable about the culture that I am proud to be a small part of).
—Website guestbook entry from Washington State

The website is also a good example of another lesson. Every program has potential to expand! For example, on the website, an enhanced version of *Alutiiq Word of the Week* allows visitors not only to hear the words featured in the radio show but to see them in print. Listeners also wanted access to proper Alutiiq pronunciations. In response, the museum posted audio files with each lesson.

Despite this step forward, the sounds of Alutiiq were missing from the gallery. An interactive touch-screen computer kiosk provided the answer. Patrons may now browse through audio *Alutiiq Word of the Week* lessons, hear the Alutiiq alphabet, and study Alutiiq grammar at a desk in the gallery. These features are also available on the museum's website and on an interactive

CD-ROM packaged with an Alutiiq alphabet poster used in a Qik'rtarmiut Alutiiq program, a three-year language immersion initiative designed to develop a new generation of fluent Alutiiq speakers. What began as a two-minute radio spot has become a lasting educational resource.

Another lesson in programming came from working with volunteers. The idea that volunteers would serve many functions in the museum wasn't practical; supervising those with little museum experience became a full-time job, creating more work for staff. And this is not even mentioning the nature of the volunteer work, which was neither educational nor exciting. Unpacking store merchandise and vacuuming involved people in the museum, but it didn't teach Alutiiq traditions or satisfy the desire for hands-on experience.

Increasing threats to Kodiak's rich archaeological record prompted the museum to evaluate and reimagine its volunteer program. With archaeological site destruction resulting from erosion, vandalism, and development on the rise, land managers began contacting the museum for assistance. Many wanted to document and preserve sites, but lacked the expertise or the staff. A Community Archaeology program was initiated to address issues of site preservation and volunteerism through an annual excavation of a threatened site near Kodiak. The focus of the program—the intensive, monthlong study of a single settlement—requires the assistance of local land managers and an excavation crew made up of community members. Participants typically work to earn internship stipends provided by Native corporations, to earn high school or college credit, or to have the opportunity to try archaeology. To supplement their field experience, the museum provides each participant with a packet of educational materials. After each season, the museum displays any excavated objects in the gallery, develops a web page, and gives both public and academic presentations on project results. Since 1995, more than 300 volunteers have given over 10,000 hours of their time to this program, and the rate of site vandalism is down. Volunteerism, public education, and historic preservation increased because the museum found a way to give volunteers a truly meaningful experience. The volunteer program became an educational program.

Evaluation

Evaluating these programs is not an easy job. How does an organization know its programs are fulfilling its mission? Quantitative measures such as collecting feedback from visitor surveys or tracking dollars raised or number of hours volunteered fail to illuminate the larger process of respect-building that the museum's public programs engender. Yet, there are signs of success.

The shelves of the museum store, once filled with Inupiaq ivory carvings and Tlingit silver jewelry, are now brimming with Alutiiq art. Accessible collections and cultural information from programs like Traveling Traditions have reawakened the arts. Change is evident when one looks at the work of a new legion of weavers, carvers, sewers, beaders, and graphic artists expressing an Alutiiq worldview.

Another positive sign is the number of young people pursuing careers in education, anthropology, community development, and the arts. The experience former program participants gained in unearthing artifacts in a muddy hole, researching an exhibit, or twining beach grass has inspired heritage-related vocations. The museum's staff is a good example. Two full-time employees were once museum interns. Today, these talented adults lead educational programs and care for objects of Alutiiq ancestry.

The museum also helped reunite the Alutiiq community. The Alaska Native Claims Settlement Act of 1971, the federal legislation that returned lands and resources to Native peoples, divided Alutiiq communities into competing corporations. Through the museum and its heritage programs, Alutiiqs now work cooperatively on activities that benefit the Native community as a whole.

Positive reception of Native culture from the Kodiak greater community has also come. The *Kodiak Daily Mirror* now publishes an annual Native Roots edition, the school district employs a full-time Alutiiq Studies Coordinator, and the tourist guide published by the Kodiak Island Convention and Visitors Bureau includes a two-page essay on Native heritage. Although the museum is not directly responsible for these advances, the awareness of Alutiiq heritage it cultivates is creating a more inclusive community history.

Recognition has also come from beyond Kodiak. In 2000, the Institute for Museum and Library Services honored the Alutiiq Museum with the National Award for Museum Service. The award recognizes three American museums that have made an outstanding effort to form community collaborations in the areas of education and historic preservation. Just five years after the museum opened, Executive Director Sven Haakanson, Jr., and I stood in the White House with President Clinton and the First Lady to accept the award on behalf of the Alutiiq Museum. This tremendous and unexpected honor encouraged the museum to move boldly forward.

Future Directions

Neither the needs of the Alutiiq community nor the programs described here are static. Although community collaborations will continue to characterize museum programs, outreach efforts will evolve to meet new challenges. Economic development is a likely focus of future projects. As Kodiak's fishing and timber industries languish, preserving and sharing Native traditions offers an alternative way of generating income. This is particularly true in rural areas where there are opportunities to develop heritage-related tourism. By creating cultural centers in rural communities, expanding opportunities to participate in archaeological research, and developing cultural events, the Alutiiq Museum can encourage economic enrichment through programming.

The museum is also starting to promote its mission by assisting small businesses. There are an increasing number of Kodiak entrepreneurs combining cultural knowledge and local resources to produce unique products—soaps, lotions, teas, knives, pottery, jewelry, basketry, clothing, and artwork. To encourage this trend, the Alutiiq Museum is leading an Alutiiq arts promotion project to encourage arts education, teach business practices, develop markets for Native-made goods, and turn the museum store into a recognized Alutiiq arts outlet. When paired with programs like Carving Traditions, museum outreach comes full circle. It not only promotes appreciation for traditional arts, but develops useful, marketable skills.

Finally, to reach deeper and more actively into the Kodiak community, the museum plans to create a public advisory committee. With the help of appointees reflecting the ethnic diversity of Kodiak, the museum will seek to identify needs that can be addressed by its mission and evaluate perceptions of the organization, the processes the museum believes are essential to sustaining its hard-won place in the Kodiak community.

NOTES

1. Ruth A. Dawson, "Endurance Through Sharing: Cultural Education and the Alutiiq Museum." Paper presented at the *Cultural Futures: Alutiiq Perspectives on Community* symposium, Anchorage Museum of History and Art, Anchorage, AK, 2003.

2. www.alutiiqmuseum.com/CarvingTraditionsIntro.htm.

3. KANA is a non-profit organization that provides healthcare and social services to Native people in the Kodiak region.

4. Rick Knecht, "Archaeology and Alutiiq Cultural Identity on Kodiak Island," in *Working Together: Native Americans & Archaeologists,* eds. K. E. Dongoske, M. Aldenderfer, and K. Doehner (Washington, D.C., Society for American Archaeology, 2002) 147–154.

5. Gordon L. Pullar, "Ethnic Identity, Cultural Pride, and Generations of Baggage: A Personal Experience," *Arctic Anthropology* 29, no. 2 (2002): 182–209.

Susan Secakuku on the Hopi Reservation. Photograph © 2003 John Harrington (Siletz). As of the spring of 2006, the Hopi Tribe continues to work toward the establishment of a tribal museum.

SUSAN SECAKUKU

CREATING MUSEUMS WITHIN A TRIBAL GOVERNMENT: A LOOK AT THE HOPI TRIBE

MUSEUMS ARE CULTURAL ORGANIZATIONS WITH AN EDUCATIONAL MISSION in promoting and preserving the arts. For the tribal museum, the mission is generally the same, but may also include the preservation of the culture and language of the tribe. Some tribal museums consider the tribal community to be their primary audience. Others anticipate their primary patrons to be non-Native visitors to the area, for whom the history of the tribe and an overview of tribal arts and culture should be presented.

The decision of whether a historical overview is necessary is but one of many decisions a tribe must consider in its plans for a museum. The tribe must also bear in mind issues such as the organizational structure and design of the museum, how building the museum will affect the tribe's government structure and laws, and how any restructuring of the tribal government might alter the operation of the museum once it opens. Museum leaders should especially stress to staff the importance of the museum's nonprofit status and how it relates to the laws and structure of the tribal government.

A museum can be created within a tribal governance structure in a variety of ways. The primary considerations for tribes in deciding what is best for them are usually sovereign immunity, taxation, and the degree of tribal council control. These issues, and the choices that arise from them, can have serious consequences for the tribe and the museum.

This essay explores the creation of a tribal museum within the context of the Hopi Tribe, outlining the tribe's optimal choices. As of 2000, at the time this article is being written, the Hopi Tribe does not have a tribal museum—that is, a museum sanctioned and owned by the tribe. (The Hopi museum that does exist, called the Hopi Cultural Center Museum, in operation since the 1970s, is private and nonprofit.)

The development of a tribal museum within the Hopi governmental structure would involve several departments of the Hopi Tribe's government. The Cultural Preservation Office (CPO), which sits within the Department of Natural Resources, currently handles all museum-related activity. Along with maintaining most research files associated with the tribe's previous museum planning projects, the department currently serves as the point of contact for the tribe's existing collection, which is stored at the Museum of Northern Arizona, as well as the repository for any new objects received by donation or through the act of repatriation. The Office of Research and Planning, which also holds records of previous projects, would assist in designing the facility and reviewing land assessments and infrastructure development.[1] The Economic Development Office would oversee any new ventures or tourism-related plans of the tribe. The Office of Legal Counsel would assist in legal protection of the entity, periodically reviewing any legal documents or issues the museum might encounter during the project. It would also assist in the development of the articles of incorporation and bylaws.[2] Certainly, the chairman, vice chairman, and tribal council members (or representatives from their offices) would be present at every step of the process. Should the museum be a true tribal corporation, the tribal council would be the governing body of the museum.

Most tribal projects begin with an idea approved by the Hopi Tribal Council for development by a steering committee and a director to oversee the conception and follow-through of all phases of the project. Tribal representatives, both governmental and nongovernmental, make up steering committees. A well-rounded committee provides representation and perspectives from various backgrounds. A steering committee for a tribal museum project might include elders and others culturally relevant, along with technicians, designers, architects, planners, lawyers, museum professionals, artists, the council chairman or his or her representative, the council vice-chairman or his or her representative, and other tribal council members. Most members would be from the Hopi community, though non-Hopi appointments are possible and should be encouraged to provide yet another perspective to this endeavor.

There are four different methods by which a Hopi tribal museum can be established under the existing Hopi tribal government structure. Outlined in the following pages are the processes, the advantages, and the issues each method brings to a museum project.

Method I—Incorporation under Hopi Ordinance 45

In 1990 the Hopi Tribal Council passed Ordinance 45 (H-45-90), titled The Hopi Tribal Governmental Corporations Act. Through its constitution, the Hopi Tribe has the legal capacity to create laws, and through Ordinance 45 it established the right to create tribal corporations. Creating a museum under this ordinance requires that the enterprise support tribal sovereignty and the powers the tribes hold to govern themselves.

The intended purpose of Ordinance 45 is to exercise and implement tribal corporate, economic, and commercial powers, which are declared by the Hopi Tribe to be of the same nature as all other tribal powers pursuant to the provisions of the constitution of the tribe. Indian tribes have been consistently recognized throughout the history of the United States as retaining governmental powers necessary to commercially utilize their resources for economic benefit and to organize corporations. This ordinance, although specifically declared for business ventures of the tribe, can also pertain to nonprofit corporations. The ordinance provides guidance for the development of a tribal museum within the tribal government structure.

Aspects of the ordinance include calling for:

- The opportunity for the museum to operate autonomously and be as self-sufficient as possible. Section 45.2 (d) clearly outlines the need for corporations established under this ordinance to be separated from other governmental functions of the tribe and to operate as tribal businesses. For purposes of efficient business management, the ordinance recognizes that management of such corporations should be based on business judgment rather than political concerns.

- Corporations to be recognized as governmental agencies and instrumentalities of the tribe. This feature grants the enterprise certain privileges and immunities by the tribe, such as immunities from suit in federal, state, and tribal courts and immunities from federal and state taxation or regulations, except as specifically set out in the corporate charters granted through this act. Corporations created under this ordinance, however, will be subject to taxation by the Hopi Tribe. At this time, there are no such corporations.

- The Hopi Tribal Council to appoint the initial incorporating directors of such corporations. The charter of the organization will govern all other elections of corporate officers and subsequent directors.

- The assets of such a corporation to be separate and distinct from those of the tribal government. However, the Hopi Tribal Council can also require that such a corporation be audited by an independent auditor, hired by the council, which has the absolute right to require access to all corporate documents necessary for the audit.

- The board of directors and management meeting to occur at least once a year, with an open meeting annually on the Hopi Reservation. The board of directors would also be required to file a full report annually of the financial and business activities of the corporation with the tribal council.

The second most important aspect of creating a museum under this ordinance is the separation of general government operations and the Hopi Tribal Council from the day-to-day management and administration of the museum. This ordinance has clearly identified the need to establish autonomous arms of the government, allowing for the establishment and administration of a board of trustees and a separate budget, yet still enabling the corporation to be immune from certain tribal situations. In tribal communities, political agendas of tribal council members can highly influence operational and personnel decisions, often to the detriment of a corporation. Tribal council members sometimes micromanage without necessarily knowing a great deal about the specifics of a corporation or project; this can sometimes lead to bad decisions, which create additional obstacles to the efficient management of programs and developments. Department heads or senior staff sometimes feel as if their hands are tied. This ordinance seems to help alleviate this potential problem.

A museum incorporated under this ordinance is still a tribal entity. Although these corporations are not considered tax-exempt through the normal federal channels—receiving the 501(c)(3) status—they can still be considered nonprofits, allowing them to receive charitable donations and apply for certain funding based on that requirement.[3] This status also allows individual donors to these organizations to receive tax deductions on their donations. This is communicated by letter from the legal counsel of the Hopi Tribe and addresses the following:[4]

- The Hopi Tribe is a federally recognized tribe.

- Section 7871 of the IRS Tax Code treats Indian tribal governments as states for certain federal tax purposes, including taxes on money for charitable contributions to the tribe or for use of a tribal government.

- The IRS tax code gives tribes state status, which is reflected in relation to income and estate tax deductions (Sections 2005 and 2106[a][2]).

- IRS Publication 526-Charitable Contributions states that Indian tribal governments or their subdivisions (i.e., the museum) that perform substantial government functions are organizations qualified to receive deductible contributions.

- IRS Revenue Procedure 83-87 provides a list of Indian tribal governments that are treated similarly to states.

- IRS Revenue Ruling 86-44 specifies that the provisions treating Indian tribal governments as states were made permanent by Section 1065 of the 1984 tax reform.

- The IRS has treated tribally incorporated entities as nonprofits.[5]

Regarding funding issues, this tax-exempt status would allow the museum to be eligible to apply for and receive grants, financial awards, or other funding opportunities. This is an important distinction to consider and clarify, because a museum is a nonprofit organization that relies heavily on outside revenue sources such as grants, member revenues, and donations. A museum is an expensive operation, and a tribe should fully understand the financial implications that running one may have on its tribal budget. In late 2002, the Institute of Museums and Library Services (IMLS), a federal program, announced that five percent of its annual budget would be dedicated to serving tribal museums. IMLS has since created a new grant program specifically for tribal museums. Award of this federal grant would require a federally recognized tribe, acting on behalf of its museum, to apply for the grant. A Hopi museum, established under Hopi Ordinance 45, would be considered a tribal entity and thus be eligible to apply for and receive awards from this source.

A museum formed under Hopi Ordinance 45 would also still be eligible for budget allocations from the tribal general operating budget, through the normal channels of a budget request.

State Taxes

Unless expressly authorized by Congress, states may not tax tribes, tribal enterprises, or tribal members for property or for activity located within the land set aside for that tribe.[6] As Congress has not subjected the Hopi Tribe to Arizona's taxation authority, and the museum will be operating within the boundaries of the Hopi Reservation, a museum would be free from state taxation.[7]

The process to create a corporation under Ordinance 45 usually begins with the development of a community steering committee, followed by the drafting and passage of a resolution by the Hopi Tribal Council. The establishment of the board of trustees occurs as part of the writing of the resolution. The articles of incorporation and the mission statement would be adopted shortly thereafter. The articles of incorporation create the entity by outlining the identity, location, powers, delegation of authority, laws, tax issues, indemnification, contracts, and assets of the organization. This is a legal document that is usually drafted with the assistance of legal counsel to assure protection of that entity. The board of trustees then creates the bylaws.

There have only been two corporations filed at Hopi under this ordinance, both of which are for-profit entities. A tribal nonprofit organization has never been created. Several private nonprofit organizations on the Hopi Reservation do exist. Discussions with those involved would be a logical step for the planners of the museum. All in all, Ordinance 45 adequately supports a museum initiative and serves as a guideline for establishing a Hopi tribal museum.

Method 2—Incorporation under IRA (1938), Section 17

A second option for the Hopi Tribe is to establish a corporation under the Indian Reorganization Act of 1938, Section 17.[8] This statute states that the Secretary of the Interior may, upon petition by any tribe, issue a charter of incorporation to such a tribe. Certain conditions apply:

- A charter shall not become operative until ratified by the governing body of such tribe.

- A charter may convey to the incorporated tribe the power to purchase, take by gift, or bequest, or otherwise own, hold, manage, operate, and dispose of property of every description, real and personal, including the power to purchase restricted Indian lands and to issue interests in corporate property in exchange thereof.

- Powers may be incidental to those of a corporation.

- No authority shall be granted to sell, mortgage, or lease for a period exceeding twenty-five years any trust or restricted lands included in the limits of the reservation.

- Any charter shall not be revoked or surrendered except by an act of Congress.

Tax Issues

There are several IRS tax code rulings on federal tax issues for corporations created under section 17 of the IRA. Revenue Rulings 94-16 and 94-65 state that a corporation organized under section 17 of the IRA is not subject to federal income tax, regardless of the location of the activities that produced the income, or whether the income was earned in the conduct of commercial business on or off the tribe's reservation.

Method 3—A Museum as a Tribal Department

A tribal museum can also be established simply as a department, office, or program under the larger Hopi tribal government structure. To determine the need for a new department and to assess its impact on staff, space, and budget, a case must be made for the museum, based on research, before the determination is made to create a museum as a new program. Should that determination be made, the next step would be to draft a resolution, which would then require the approval of the tribal council.

Today, the Hopi Tribe's Cultural Preservation Office (CPO) sits under the Department of Natural Resources and is responsible for all current museum-related activity. Preliminary findings could determine that if a museum were established through these channels, a new program under the Department of Natural Resources might not be created, but a new "project" within the CPO could be created.

Although this method is not in the Hopi Tribe's experience, there is another tribe that has established a museum by this way. Its tribal council established this museum. Administratively, it is a cultural resources department within their tribal government. The potential problems with this model of creating a tribal museum are explained below.

First, the director and staff of this department are not only responsible for museum-related functions but also for other cultural programs, such as the language program, archives, archaeological mapping, etc. Other U.S. tribes have chosen to create these programs as entities separate from a museum. For one existing tribal museum, it is problematic that the director and staff answer directly to the tribal council, instead of to a board of directors. The director of that museum states, "The council did not and continues to not fully understand the various aspects of museum operations. The museum and the rest of my department is only one of many departments they [the council] oversee, and we seem to be always at the bottom of the list." It would seem that there is little focus on, attention to, or support of the museum by this tribe's governing council. Also, it would be easier in this situation for the decisions or actions regarding the museum, as well as other programs the tribal council manages, to be politicized. This museum also receives a majority of its operating budget from the tribal fund, so every year the director must submit a budget request, which is not necessarily guaranteed favorable action. A unique element of the community of this particular museum and its government is size. Because the government is relatively small, it does not have in-house legal counsel. Instead, it contracts with a law firm that deals only with the tribal council. Therefore, any legal assistance needed by the museum must be requested by the museum director and submitted to the tribal council. The council then determines if it will take the issue to its legal counsel.[9]

There are some instances in this example that do not relate to the Hopi tribal scenario, but the example of a museum having to answer to a tribal council versus a board of directors is clear. Another issue centers around the fact that, having no nonprofit federal tax status (known as 501[c][3] status), a museum is thus ineligible to apply for and receive certain kinds of funding. If a museum is a department, it is not considered an incorporated business enterprise of the tribe. For tax purposes, it would be treated similarly to a corporation established along the lines of those found in Method Two. In like manner, federal and state taxes would not be applied as long as the entity was located on the reservation.

There are two key issues to consider when following this method. First, the museum is not considered a chartered organization, and therefore does not have the federal tax status that would make it eligible for certain kinds of funding and tax breaks. Second, direct tribal council oversight or lack thereof creates a variety of contentious issues. For the Hopi Tribe, if a museum were created under the CPO, the museum director would report to the CPO director, who would report to the Department of Natural Resource director, who would in turn report to the council. This structure creates more levels of hierarchy and does not provide the focused direction that a board of trustees would, and is much more subject to political pressure.

Method 4—Incorporation through the State of Arizona

Incorporation can also be created through the state in which the corporation will reside. In case of the Hopi Tribe, Arizona would be the state to be considered. This process includes filing articles of incorporation with the Arizona State Corporation Commission. Most non-tribal museums within the United States are incorporated through the state in which they are located.

The decision for tribes to incorporate through their state subjects the tribe to state taxes and other state regulations. Tribal sovereignty conveys a certain status that can equate tribes to states in many circumstances. By using this method, tribes would risk waiving their sovereign status. In addition, other tax repercussions, outlined below, may come into play. For these reasons, tribes should seriously consider incorporation through a state as the absolute last alternative. Should a tribe be interested in filing for nonprofit incorporation through the state of Arizona, however, the steps include:

- Corporation name: Verify the entity name for availability and get a copy of the trade name certificate. A certificate of disclosure with signature(s) of all incorporators and dated within thirty days of delivery to the commission must also be provided.

- Articles of incorporation: This document should indicate the proposed name of the corporation, the initial business/affairs, the street address of the known place of business in Arizona (may be in care of the address of the statutory agent—if agent, cannot be a P.O. box), the name and address of the statutory agent (cannot be a P.O. box), the applicable tax-exemption code, the name(s) and address(es) of the initial board of directors (minimum of one), and the name(s) and address(es) of the incorporators (minimum of one). Applicants must also indicate whether the corporation will or will not have members and must include signatures of all incorporators and the signature of statutory agent (acknowledging acceptance).

- Fees: A filing fee of $40, made payable to the commission, is required for nonprofit organizations.

- Publication: A copy of the articles of incorporation must be published in a newspaper of general circulation, in the county of the known place of business in Arizona, for three (3) consecutive publications. This should not be published until the documents are approved. Applicants must file an affidavit of publication with the commission.

More detailed information on this particular process can be found at the Arizona State Corporation Commission. Similar offices are found in all states.

Federal Tax-Exempt Status for State-Organized Corporations by Tribes

Corporations that do not qualify for tax-exempt status through the actions mentioned in Method One must qualify for it through the normal procedures. Those legally constituted not-for-profit corporations that have been set up to serve a public purpose can be tax-exempt, according to the IRS. However, they must have the following characteristics:

- A public service mission;

- Organization as a not-for-profit or charitable corporation;

- Governance structures that preclude self-interest and private financial gain;

- Exemption from paying federal tax;

- Possession of special legal status that stipulates gifts made to them are tax-deductible.

The following federal applications would be required to receive tax exemptions, an employer identification number, and an exempt organization letter from the Internal Revenue Service:

1. IRS Form 1023: Application for Recognition of Exemption Under Section 501(c)(3) of the Internal Revenue Service;

2. IRS Form 872-C: Consent Fixing Period of Limitation Upon Assessment of Tax under Section 4940 of the Internal Revenue Code;

3. SS-4: Application for Employer Identification Number (EIN);

4. Form 8718: User Fee for Exempt Organization Determination Letter Request.

The following IRS Publications are available for more information:

- Publication 557—*Tax-Exempt Status for Your Organization;*

- Publication 598—*Tax on Unrelated Business Income of Exempt Organizations.*

Certain IRS rulings can also affect tribal corporations created under state law. Revenue Ruling 94-16 states that corporations organized by an Indian tribe under state law are subject to federal tax on their income, regardless of the location of the activity that produced it. It is not certain if this applies to nonprofit corporations. If so, it is also not clear if this would be considered income of the museum or unrelated income. These would be good enough reasons to do more legal research, and, possibly, have a tribe consider not creating an organization under the state.

Summary

Creating a corporation under the state is a tribe's least desirable option for several reasons. As sovereign entities, tribes have the legal power to create corporations, and this power should be exercised. By creating an organization through the state, however, they waive this power. Another reason tribes should avoid state incorporation is to protect themselves from subjection to state law and rules, including tax rulings.

Several attorneys who work for tribes or for firms that focus on tribal law have mentioned in discussions with this author that they highly advise any tribe against state incorporation because of sovereignty and tax issues. Tribes that are considering opening a new tribal museum will have to explore these issues within the context of their own tribal and state laws. By exploring this issue within the context of the Hopi Tribe, however, one can begin to understand how decisions in the creation of a museum as a tribal entity can affect the daily operation and growth of such an institution; one can also find throughout tribal communities examples of effective decision-making among successful tribal entities. Tribal museums are storehouses of cultural material, voices of contemporary tribal communities, showcases of old and new art, and centers for cultural programs that lead to preservation of cultural traditions and tribal values, and time should be spent on determining how best to allow these organizations to thrive and contribute to their communities.

NOTES

1. Michael Kelly, Principal Planner, Hopi Tribe Office of Research and Planning. Interview by author, April 10, 2000.

2. Lisa Estensen, Assistant General Counsel, Hopi Tribe. Interview by author, April 10, 2000.

3. Estensen, interview.

4. Estensen, interview.

5. Estensen, interview.

6. *Mescalero Apache Tribe v. Jones*, 411 U.S. 145 (1973).

7. Shawn Frank, Esq., Nordhaus, Haltom, Taylor, Taradash, and Frye. Interview by author, April 21, 2000.

8. Estensen, interview.

9. Telephone conversation with unnamed museum director, April 12, 2000.

RESOURCES

Ambrose, Timothy. *Managing New Museums: A Guide to Good Practice*. Edinburg: Scottish Museums Council, 1993.

Canby, William C. *American Indian Law in a Nutshell*. St. Paul, MN: West Publishing, 1998.

Conor, T. "Controlling Instruments of the Nonprofit Organization: ByLaws and the Articles of Incorporation." In *The Nonprofit Handbook*, 1986.

Estensen, Lisa, Assistant General Counsel, the Hopi Tribe. Interview by author. April 10, 2000.

Frank, Shawn, Esq., Nordhaus, Haltom, Taylor, Taradash, and Frye. Interview by author. April 21, 2000.

Ingram, Richard T. "Ten Basic Responsibilities of Non-Profit Boards." Washington, DC: National Center for Non-Profit Boards, 1988.

Kelly, Michael, Principal Planner, Hopi Tribe Office of Research and Planning. Interview by author. April 10, 2000.

Malaro, Marie. *Museum Governance: Mission, Ethics, and Policy*. Washington, DC: The Smithsonian Institution Press, 1994.

Ullberg, Alan, and Patricia Ullberg. "Museum Trusteeship." Washington, DC: American Association of Museums, 1981.

Wolf, Thomas. *Managing a Nonprofit Organization in the Twenty-First Century*. New York: Simon & Schuster, 1999.

Bureau of Indian Affairs, United States Department of Interior. Website: www.doi.gov.

Janine Bowechop, director of the Makah Cultural and Research Center, stands at the museum entrance. Photograph courtesy of MCRC.

JEFFREY E. MAUGER AND JANINE BOWECHOP

TRIBAL COLLECTIONS MANAGEMENT AT THE MAKAH CULTURAL AND RESEARCH CENTER

SOME 300 YEARS AGO, A CATASTROPHIC MUD SLIDE buried at least four houses in the Makah winter village of Ozette, near the northwest tip of what is now known as Washington State. While destructive, the slide also created conditions that protected wood and plant fiber artifacts, materials that are typically not well preserved on the Northwest Coast. As a result, nearly a decade of archaeological excavations at the site yielded some 55,000 artifacts and 15,000 structural remains of the four houses. The excavation of the site, by archaeological teams composed of both Makah and University of Washington students, ended in 1981. To exhibit the collections, in 1979 the Makah Tribe founded the Makah Cultural and Research Center (MCRC) in Neah Bay, Washington, where the main village on the Makah Reservation is located.

In 1993, with the opening of a new curatorial facility and the transfer of management and housing of artifacts to the Ozette Archaeological Collection, the MCRC inherited the organizational system developed for archaeological research purposes. As such, access to the collection was through conventional archaeological artifact categories. Artifacts were stored as functionally related groups in broad technological categories; sealing and whaling gear, for example, was located under a general category of "sea mammal hunting gear," boxes and bowls as subdivisions of "containers," and wedges and chisels under "woodworking." Management of the collection was carried out by MCRC employees, and other access was based on research needs. While this system made the artifacts available for study, it failed to reflect Makah values and cultural concerns centering around traditional property rights and sanctions concerning the handling of certain items; at best, it was neutral to such values and concerns and, at worst, it disregarded them.

The construction of a new curatorial facility in 1993 provided the opportunity for developing a system that allows for the care of and access to the collection, in addition to reflecting the values and concerns of the Makah people. With the installation of the Ozette collection in the new curatorial facility, a computer-based inventory of the collection was initiated, allowing access to individual objects and groups of artifacts. The MCRC collections staff also acknowledged and took into account a number of cultural concerns connected with the management of the Ozette collection.

Social Units

Each of the buried Ozette houses represented an extended family or household, with several related nuclear families organized under a single head. Property within each house belonged to the occupants—either individuals, nuclear families, or the household as a corporate unit. While developing a collections management system for the new facility, the collections staff was gently reminded that the traditional system of the ownership of property, both tangible and intangible, still exists in the Neah Bay community. Consequently, the staff began separating and storing Ozette artifacts not only within artifact categories, but also by the households from which they were recovered. While space limitations precluded storing all the contents of one house separate from the others, household designations were incorporated in the shelf labeling. For example, while all spindle whorls were stored together, they were separated and labeled within their storage area by household designation.

Janine Bowechop with a bowl that survived the Ozette mud slide.
Photograph courtesy of MCRC.

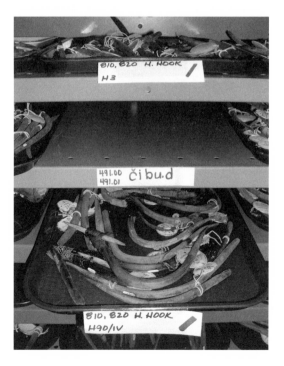

Inexpensive trays and containers
have been used to manage the
MCRC collection. Photograph
courtesy of MCRC.

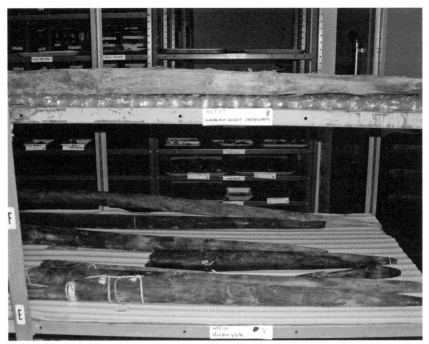

Storage labels at the MCRC use both Makah language and English. Photograph courtesy of MCRC.

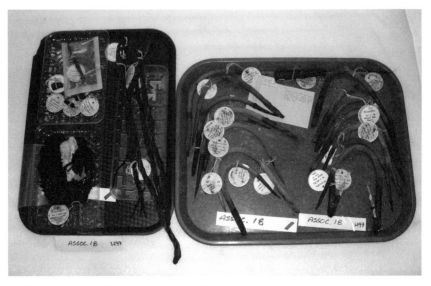

Artifacts in storage. Photograph courtesy of MCRC.

Personal Property

Because of the way the buried houses and their contents were preserved, the property of specific individuals could be recognized in the Ozette collection through their association in containers such as boxes and baskets; often these were functionally related artifacts such as a fishing pouch that contained finished hooks, bone splinters for fashioning barbs, a whetstone for sharpening barbs, and leader material (raw materials for making the fishing line). In some cases, baskets of material were located within other baskets that were stored within a larger basket. Following the traditional concepts, the associations have been identified and the objects have been reassembled; they are now stored together as a unit.

Gender Restrictions

In traditional Makah society, certain gender restrictions were applied to the handling of some tools. Whaling gear, for example, could not be touched or handled by women below a certain age. Because values such as these were traditionally associated with the Ozette artifacts and are still held in varying degrees in the Makah community, the shelves containing these artifacts are flagged with symbols indicating a gender restriction. These restrictions apply to staff, researchers, and visitors alike. The imposition of gender restrictions in MCRC collections management defined the need for both male and female curators in the MCRC. It also suggested areas of Makah culture requiring further documentation. Paralleling the bias in much of the ethnographic literature, information on Makah gender restrictions is much more available for men's objects, although, clearly, some women's tools are likely to have been restricted from use by men. Future efforts on the part of the MCRC collections staff will be focused on documenting traditional values and the degree to which they are still held in the Makah community.

Makah Language

One of the major mission goals of the MCRC is to support the preservation and use of Makah language. Consequently, the collections staff began labeling artifacts in both Makah and English. A major innovation was the physical grouping of artifacts according to their Makah roots and/or suf-fixes. In Makah, for example, containers are indicated by the suffix /sac/. The Makah name for such boxes, however, lacks this suffix despite the fact that they clearly functioned as containers; rather, their Makah name refers to the unique woodworking technique of kerfed and bent corners. In Makah, then, the technology of the boxes seems to have been more significant in naming them than their function. Consequently, these boxes were stored apart from, rather than with, bowls and other containers. After making the distinction between boxes and actual containers, the next logical step was to examine the remainder of the collection to determine whether anything else is described as a container in the Makah language. Interestingly, the name for the cedar dugout canoes for which the Makahs are famous con-tains the /sac/ suffix and translates into English as "containers for people." In Makah nomenclature, then, canoes have a relationship to baskets and bowls, while boxes do not.

Thus, physically storing and labeling the Ozette collection according to Makah language encouraged analysis of the cultural meanings and affini-ties between artifacts in the collection and provides insight into both Makah language and thought. Another example is provided by wedges, chisels, canoe paddles, and adzes. They appear to share the same root, and when physi-cally grouped together, these artifacts were seen to have been classified lin-guistically by their manner of use, rather than their actual use or function. This kind of collections management system, then, not only provides an organizing device for accessing information and artifacts, but a tool for re-flecting, understanding, and preserving the cognitive system within which the artifacts were produced and used.

Today, the curatorial facility of the Makah Cultural and Research Center responds to both museological and tribal collections concerns. Artifacts are housed in a modern, environmentally controlled, and secure storage facility, and information on them is provided by a computer-based data management system. This system, however, responds to concerns of collections manage-ment both within and outside the Makah community. Handling and stor-age of the collection are based on both accepted museum practice and the

Janine Bowechop and an Ozette box in the MCRC collections storage area. Photograph courtesy of MCRC.

traditional values of the Makah people. This system, then, supports Makah culture rather than eroding it. Moreover, the use of Makah language in organizing the artifacts allows insights into the culture that produced them.

The ways in which tribal collections are stored, managed, and accessed may have profound significance to their host communities as agents of preservation and support or as agents of change. At the MCRC, the merging of tribal values and concerns with the management of the collection has resulted in a truly tribal appropriate collections management system.

RESOURCES

Daugherty, Richard, and Ruth Kirk. "Ancient Indian Village Where Time Stood Still." *Smithsonian Magazine* 7, no. 2 (1976): 68–75.

Kirk, Ruth. *Hunters of the Whale*. New York: William Morrow and Company, 1974.

Kirk, Ruth, and Richard Daugherty. *Exploring Washington Archaeology*. Seattle and London: University of Washington Press, 1978.

Pasqua, Maria Parker. "Ozette in 1491: America Before Columbus." *National Geographic* 180, no. 4 (October 1991): 38–53.

Tweedie, Ann M. *Drawing Back Culture: The Makah Struggle for Repatriation*. Seattle: University of Washington Press, 2002.

Irvine J. Scalplock holding a Siksika split-horn headdress, made in 1958 by Augustine Yellow Sun. The Siksika Museum must create individual boxes for each object in the collection in preparation for the move to the new interpretive center at Blackfoot Crossing Historical Park. The facility opens in the spring of 2006. Photograph by Michelle Crow Chief, courtesy of the Siksika Museum.

IRVINE J. SCALPLOCK

Tribal Museums and the Siksika Experience

For First Nations of Canada (this term became preferable to "Indian" in Canada in the 1970s), tribal museums and cultural centers are an effective arena in which to fight the misguided notion that indigenous people are vanishing. One tribal museum, the Siksika Museum, established in 1967 in Alberta, houses five collections of ethnographic material.

Siksika means "Blackfoot." The Siksika people, one of four First Nations groups belonging to the Blackfoot Confederacy, live on reservations in northern Montana and on reserved lands in southern Alberta. By the late nineteenth century, white settlers, disease, warfare, and the near extinction of bison herds needed for subsistence had decimated Blackfoot Indians. Today, Siksika members number approximately 4,700 in Alberta, while another 9,000 Blackfoot live on and around reserved lands in Montana.

Material that dates to the 1800s can be found in the small community-based Siksika Museum. Located in the community's old residential school, the museum operates out of three rooms—storage, exhibit area, and office. The 1926 building, which stands as a solemn reminder of the residential school period, houses the Old Sun Community College and the education library, as well as the Siksika Museum. The material from the collection was acquired from the Siksika community between the late 1950s and the early 1970s.

The increased visibility of cultural centers and tribal museums such as the Siksika Museum, and the active roles Natives are now playing in the interpretation of their material culture, highlight issues of the exhibition, handling, and repatriation of objects, as well as issues of accessible collections and museum training. For decades, Native owners of the material culture that furnished museum exhibits had little, if any, say in the treatment of objects in museum care, nor did they possess the means to have their cultural items returned to them. But as the attitude toward the presentation of Native cultures changed, all museums—whether tribal or non-tribal, national or local—would be confronted with dilemmas in displaying and returning Native objects, especially those of a religious nature.

Despite the museum community's general oversight and underrepresentation of First Nations' perspectives, progress has been made. An important step in the effective collaboration of Canadian museums and First Nations groups came with the formation of advisory boards to address the growing demands of repatriation. Mutual respect of cultures led to the creation of the boards, which are made up of individuals from local First Nations communities who act as representatives. This relationship with non-Native or "mainstream" museums was not without its problems. Who has the authority to speak about traditional knowledge? How factual is the information? The overarching goal of advisory boards is to bridge the knowledge gap between Western and Native ideas to more accurately determine what is and isn't acceptable in an exhibition.

In 2001 Alberta's passage of the First Nations Sacred Ceremonial Objects Repatriation Act allowed for the return of religious artifacts to their owners. In 1996, nine Horn Society ceremonial bundles were returned to the Siksika people. Eight more bundles have since been recovered through repatriation. Not coincidentally, the Horn Societies have increased in membership, and a revival of traditional teachings and practices has followed. In the case of ceremonial bundles, their content may vary from tribe to tribe and person to person and with a tribe's or person's spiritual beliefs. Differences aside, they are powerful objects and their return has had profound effects on their communities.

For Alberta museums, new circumstances arose under the laws of repa-
ration. In some cases, for example, a lost bundle that was sold or given to a
museum would be subject to repatriation. Some bundles have been known
to circulate among tribes of the same tongue. In such cases of communal
ownership, to whom would the bundles be returned? Where once tribes or
groups requested the return of cultural items, individuals now made requests
for the return of material formerly possessed by family members. As issues
of authority arose, the conflict between Native knowledge and western ideas
became apparent.

To ensure the appropriateness of the process—that an individual or group
has legitimate claim to an object—advisory boards, composed of members
of sacred societies, must determine where and to whom the object can be
repatriated. These requests are treated on a case-by-case basis. Also, the return of items from museum collections is not meant to jeopardize the integrity of these collections. Only materials significant to ritual and ceremony are considered for repatriation. This premise is clearly understood by
the museums and First Nations communities.

The presence of advisory boards also changed policy regarding collections. An object the museum professional may classify as a cultural artifact
may also, to the Native, hold sacred beliefs and require care within Native
tradition. To the Blackfoot, sacred items require spiritual cleansing. Sacred
objects are likened to children, and need to be treated with respect and rev-
erence. Given greater accessibility to collections, the Blackfoot were able to
go into collections and traditionally smudge their ceremonial material.
"Smudging" is the burning of sweetgrass in a blessing. In designated smudging areas in museums, smoke alarms are disabled and elders may offer the
blessing. Bundles must be smudged daily with sweetgrass and kept in quiet
places away from noise and disturbances. For traditional people this is very
important, as some of the ceremonial bundles are still considered very powerful. Making collections accessible has led not only to repatriation, but also
to the successful revival of Sun Dances and Medicine Pipe ceremonies. Also,
in Alberta it is not uncommon to see museum professionals at ceremonies,
their faces painted with ocher. Because of the powerful nature of the cere-

monial bundles, museum professionals are encouraged to participate in ceremonies to ensure their safety and to help them understand the significance of holy bundles.

Museum conservators often worry that artifacts used ceremonially may be physically mishandled and damaged, when, in fact, careful attention goes into granting ceremonial rights to handlers. Only by traditional transferring ceremonies do individuals attain the right to handle certain objects. The reality is, however, that mainstream museums and tribal museums have yet to set a course to accommodate First Nations lifeviews and perspectives. And because Native methods of care are fundamentally at odds with Western methods, even the most thoughtful exhibition planning can be met with the First Nations visitor who believes the ceremonial bundle has been mishandled or the pipe on exhibition has been displayed improperly. In the tug-of-war between Native and Western methodologies, it's important that the museums and their Native counterparts resolve differences without compromising the integrity of the object.

In the case of Blackfoot bundles, it is clear that their accessibility and their return contributed to religious continuance and opened dialogue between museum professionals and Blackfoot peoples. For the lines of communication between museum professionals and First Peoples to remain open, mutual understanding of cultures should be a learning imperative for museum professionals, Native and non-Native alike. Ideally, having staff from First Nations can aid in "educating" museum personnel on Native perspectives. In keeping with accepted museum practices, all staff are trained in the Western techniques of preservation and conservation, and Canadian museums offer training programs for First Nations.

It is critical for established institutions to create museum study programs for Natives. In 1994 a pilot project was formed at the Canadian Museum of Civilization in Hull, Quebec, to provide training in museum study. For a period of eight months, interns worked in different departments in the fields of ethnology, conservation, technical services, research, school programs, and security and protection services. At the conclusion of the training, the interns received a certificate of participation in and completion of

The design of the Blackfoot Crossing interpretive center resembles a painted tipi laid out on the ground, forming a half-circle. The seven cones on the roof represent the seven warrior societies of the Siksika. Photograph by Michelle Crow Chief, courtesy of the Siksika Museum.

the program. Programs like this one are invaluable to First Nations people who are interested in pursuing museum-related professions and invaluable to the museum community whose mission is to serve First Peoples.

The Siksika museum's first curator, Russell Wright, understood that education was indispensable to creating a museum environment. Though Wright had been trained to be a curator, he admirably took on several roles, including cultural coordinator, historian, and Blackfoot language instructor. Although funding wasn't always available for conservation materials, staff kept reports on the condition of the collections continuously updated, monitored the environment, and applied traditional conservation methods.

By the early 1980s, the Siksika people began to see the tourist potential of Siksika Nation. In 1989, the Blackfoot Crossing Development project failed due to lack of funding and support, but the spirit of the project was to signal the development of the Blackfoot Crossing Interpretive Center. As this idea began to take hold, so too did the idea of a tribal museum. There were many debates about museums versus interpretive centers. The arguments surrounding the new construction were debated even as the ground gave way for the new interpretive center/museum. But the inarguable facts were clear: the Siksika Museum had evolved to become a learning institution, and the material culture of the Siksika people would be preserved for generations to come.

Interior of the Suquamish Museum. Photograph by Marilyn Jones, courtesy of the Suquamish Tribal Archives.

MARILYN G. JONES

Building the Suquamish Museum

I have been asked to share some thoughts with you on how to build a tribal museum. This is a task that involves love, respect, honor, and a desire to share with as many as possible the history and culture of a people.

I am one of approximately one thousand Suquamish tribal members. In the late 1960s our tribe decided to build a museum to preserve, protect, and educate people on Suquamish culture and history. With help from consultants, funding agencies, and a commercial loan from a local bank, two young women, along with a tribal member who was both a curator and archivist, began collecting and identifying photographs and artifacts and contacting elders to make this dream a reality. Through community interest, grants, and careful planning, the Suquamish Tribal Cultural Center was created. Designated as 501(c)(3) under federal tax code, our organization received nonprofit status and thus became eligible for tax benefits.

Some of the sources approached in our successful effort to fund the museum were:

- National Endowment for the Humanities;

- National Endowment for the Arts;

- The Bullet Foundation;

- VISTA Volunteer Programs (Volunteer in Service to America);

- Western Washington Indian Employment Training Program, JTPA (Job Training Partnership Act), WEX (Work Experience), and OJT (On-the-Job Training);

- Small Tribes Organization of Western Washington, CETA (Comprehensive Employment Training Act), JTPA, WEX, and OJT;

- North Sound Bank;

- Bureau of Indian Affairs;

- and the Suquamish Tribe.

The Suquamish Tribe's new tribal center was near completion when it burned to the ground. But with assistance from Seattle's Museum of History and Industry, the Burke Museum, the Seattle Art Museum, and many others, the Suquamish Tribe and tribal center staff opened *The Eyes of Chief Seattle* at the Seattle Museum of History and Industry. Following a one-year run, the exhibit was translated into French and sent to Seattle's sister city of Nantes, France, for another year. In the meantime, the bank loan came in, and tribal members worked tirelessly on the new center. On June 1, 1983, *The Eyes of Chief Seattle* opened at the Suquamish Tribal Center. Through exhibits that used resources such as oral history, photo archives, and artifacts loaned to us from other museums, a dream came true.

We have three publications, which were developed after the collection processes were nearly complete. They are:

1. *The Suquamish Tribal Photographic Archives Project: A Case Study*

2. *A Guide for Oral History in the Native American Community*

3. *The Eyes of Chief Seattle: Exhibit Catalogue*

For the Oral History Project, we hired three oral history interviewers to go into the community and record some of our oral traditions. Upon completion of the Oral History Project, we selected quotes and placed them throughout the exhibit to bring the photographs and artifacts to life. We also developed a slide show in 1983 called *Come Forth Laughing: Voices of the Suquamish People.* This show won the Silver Screen Award for Outstanding Creativity in the Production of Audio/Visual Communications in International Competition from the U.S. Industrial Film Festival in 1984.

The following are traveling exhibits:
1. *Suquamish People: Legacy and Transition*
2. *100 Years of Photography: Selections from the Suquamish Tribal Archives*
3. *Suquamish Elder* (video also available)

Our cultural education programs include:
1. Suquamish Basketry
2. Suquamish Tribal History
3. We Are the Suquamish

All of these are used to assist in the understanding of the culture and history of the Suquamish Tribe and were developed by museum staff. We worked very closely with our community and schools to ensure that the projects would be of the highest educational value to people of all ages and backgrounds. And today, as I work in the museum and hear the comments of guests from around the world, I cannot help but feel a swell of pride in the work of so many of us to make the dream of our elders come true. We will continue to keep it growing into the future for our youth to share with the generations to come.

My advice if you are considering starting a tribal museum is:

1. Start with a well thought-out plan.
2. Meet with consultants and other museum professionals.
3. Ask questions. Dig for the unexpected in attics, basements, town libraries, churches, schools, and through word of mouth. Have a secure place to inventory and label everything.
4. Develop a cataloguing system, and make sure everyone knows how to use it.
5. Keep paper, computer, and photographic records of each and every item, regardless of size, shape, or style.
6. Insure everything and get legal descriptions in full detail to your insurance company.
7. Plan exhibits that tell a story and excite you and your visitors.
8. Develop both hands-on and electronic educational materials for schools.
9. Try to show all sides of history and events to trigger questions and provoke visitors to learn more.
10. Seek books and other materials that will encourage visitors to continue to learn.
11. Survey your community and others for feedback on your exhibit.
12. Elders and families of your tribe are your best resources.
13. Hold dinners and luncheons to share your ideas.
14. Raise money through memberships and auctions.
15. Always remember that your goals and accomplishments are as important to the community as they are to the people employed by the museum.

If you build with love, respect, honor, and a desire to share, your museum will come true and be beautiful.

Marilyn Jones holding a drum by David A. Boxley (Tsimshian), painted by his son, David R. Box-ley. The drum's design features a family portrait of Jones, her husband, and their children. Photo-graph by Lorene Boxley (Tlingit), courtesy of the Suquamish Tribal Archives.

Exhibition on local religious customs at Yukuni'i, a community museum in San José Chichihualtepec, 2003. Photograph by Carolin Kollewe.

CUAUHTÉMOC CAMARENA AND TERESA MORALES

The Power of Self-Interpretation:
Ideas on Starting a Community Museum

Since 1985, both authors of this essay have been actively supporting rural indigenous communities of the southern state of Oaxaca, Mexico, in the creation and development of community museums.[1] Throughout the years, fourteen museums in Mixteco, Zapoteco, Chocholteco, and Mestizo communities have opened their doors to the public. The state association of community museums, Unión de Museos Comunitarios de Oaxaca, has developed a training center, a cooperative for community tourism, and a dynamic exchange program with other community museums throughout Mexico and tribal museums in Arizona. The association has also worked in Guatemala, El Salvador, Nicaragua, Costa Rica, Panama, Venezuela, Ecuador, and Bolivia, where communities are creating and strengthening their museums.[2]

Throughout this process, both of us have very much enjoyed the opportunity to meet with a wide variety of community representatives from different countries, with whom we have discussed the importance of community museums and the processes by which they are developed. This article sums up some of the general considerations at work in initiating a community museum and some methods to make this process easier.

First, a working definition of a community museum—especially how it differs from a traditional, mainstream museum—can be understood as a museum that develops around a collection of objects, a team of experts, a building, and its public.[3] In contrast, the birth of a community museum is a community initiative; it responds to local needs and demands, is directed by a community organization, and is created and developed with the direct involvement of the local population. The community is the owner of the museum, whose work strengthens community organization and action beyond its walls.[4]

To appreciate the potential of the community museum, consider the challenges local communities, especially disadvantaged ones, face today. The effects of globalization include persistent poverty, loss of cultural identity, accelerated migration, and disintegration of the bonds of unity and solidarity within local communities.[5] In this context, the community museum is not a luxury, and its value is not simply decorative: it is a necessity that allows communities to repossess their heritage, both physically and symbolically. It is a tool for rethinking the future, for facing rapid transformations with the strength born of a core identity rooted in the past. It is a concrete image of the values that bind a people together, and a vehicle to project and legitimize these values. It is an opportunity to remember the vital experiences that should not be forgotten, but should be preserved to educate the generations who will inherit them.

As a repository for the stories a community tells to recreate its way of life, the community museum is a process of self-interpretation. In the museum, community members participate collectively in selecting themes for exhibitions, in choosing and collecting objects, in researching and analyzing their history and culture, in representing their stories, and in creating drawings, murals, photographs, scale models, and life-size installations. In this process, all participants are dynamically engaged, strengthening and developing direct personal bonds to their collective identity. They also have the opportunity to share a learning experience, to step back and collectively analyze the elements of community unity and conflict through creative interpretation.

These museums are also centers for cultural organization and action that mobilize a community and provoke it to develop new initiatives. They generate programs to strengthen the cultural identity of children, train adults in a variety of skills, promote and support local artists and artisans, and develop community tourism. Community museums are a window on the world, offering multiple possibilities for cultural exchange as well as serving as a vehicle for networking with other communities. These networks between communities allow local initiatives to expand and become regional in scope, affecting cultural policies by making the voice of communities heard.

The first steps taken to create a museum with these characteristics can

Community assembly electing a new museum committee, Cerro Marín, April 2004. Photograph by Cuauhtémoc Camarena.

vary greatly from case to case, but a common thread is the initial establishment of community ownership of the project. The beginning of the museum is rooted within the community to develop an inclusive decision-making process and build the vision and organization that will allow the community to be in charge of the project. The first actions carried out in this direction will be vital if local involvement is to continue growing.

For this first initiative to be born, some individuals within the community must launch and promote the idea. Sometimes they are local authorities, community leaders, teachers, or common citizens. Gradually, these initiators help generate enthusiasm and begin to establish a working group. In some cases, they constitute a group within the community that is already recognized as legitimately representing local concerns. In other instances, they comprise a newly established, informal group of volunteers.

In communities where there is a broadly recognized decision-making body that sanctions all important community projects, such as the village assembly, the community meeting, or the tribal council, the next step is to pres-

Group activity during a meeting of the Union of Community Museums of Oaxaca, San José el Mogote, 1993. Photograph by Cuauhtémoc Camarena.

ent the proposal of the museum project for community approval. The requirements the initiators must fulfill in order to gain this approval vary greatly from case to case. This step could entail clarifying the idea of the museum, convincing local authorities to present the proposal for consideration, and disseminating the proposal widely among the local population. When such decision-making processes are clearly in place, the task of generating consensus community approval is made much easier.

In communities where such grassroots decision-making bodies do not exist, the initiators of the project must seek to generate community ownership by establishing links to a wide variety of local organizations, groups, and individuals. In this process, the working group usually needs to become more formal and structured, and often must acquire legal status as an association or nongovernmental organization. The most successful associations of this kind are able to expand to include representatives of important community organizations and groups. Although they are not required to go through a formal process to achieve community approval, they face a greater challenge: to find their own way to build community consensus, creatively inventing and promoting a wide variety of activities and programs.[6] In the cases where a community has approved the museum project through its main decision-making body, it is advantageous for this same body to elect or appoint a committee to coordinate the effort. In some communities, this is the normal procedure after project approval. In this way, the committee or working team, as a legitimate group of community representatives, has an excellent degree of public recognition and moral authority to begin to promote the museum project.

In both cases, what was an incipient idea must turn into a shared community concern, and what started out as a few interested people must turn into a structured working team. The museum project will become a shared concern when enough people in the community feel that they have been consulted, listened to, and involved in concrete activities. They need to feel that their opinion has weight, through their participation in large community meetings, through discussions in local associations and organizations (schools, youth groups, organizations of artists and artisans, neighborhood associations, etc.), through surveys, and through door-to-door consultations. They also need to be invited to participate in various contests, donation campaigns, interviews, workshops, lectures, community festivals, and small temporary exhibits, to name a few activities. The working team, on the other hand, must develop its capacity to plan, coordinate, and carry out these activities.

After collective discussion of the proposal and the decision to create the museum, several basic issues emerge that offer excellent opportunities to continue community consultations. What should the museum speak of? What stories should it tell? What parts of its history, culture, and present situation does the community want to represent, research, and learn about? Often the first initiators of the museum have specific ideas of what the museum should address, but the voice of the rest of the community should be heard if it is to become a collective project.

Where should the museum be located? This is another decision that involves allocating certain community resources in terms of its public areas and infrastructure. Community members will appreciate having a say as to how this aspect of the project can be resolved, instead of being informed after the decision has been made.

Once the community has expressed its support of the museum project, spoken out about what issues the museum should address, and given its opinion about where the museum should be built, the museum committee or association has a strong foundation to continue the process of community engagement. At this point, there are several tasks that must be addressed almost simultaneously. These include the ongoing process of training and promotion among community members, the creation of the exhibitions and collections, the planning and installation of the building, and the development of support networks with other museums, organizations, and communities. Thus, the museum committee must develop a work plan that takes these different aspects into account.[7]

As this stage begins, planners need to recognize two important focal points of community training: the museum committee and the community workshops. The museum committee must continue to clarify its vision of the community museum and to complete a planning process to develop the different phases of the project in a fashion that continuously enhances community ownership. Workshops must develop participatory techniques that will allow the community to express its concerns in the exhibitions to be created.

The process of creating the exhibition involves conceptualization, research, and documentation; development of the collection, script, and design; and production and installation. Each one of these phases offers opportunities to organize workshops and involve community members. It is particularly significant to achieve community participation in the conceptualization and research phases, where the basic ideas and orientation of the exhibition will be defined. Oral history workshops are an excellent tool for inviting community members to interview and record the experience of other community members, to share and preserve significant stories.[8]

Planning the building and the exhibitions to be installed is a task the museum committee must develop in collaboration with the local authorities, usually seeking advice from professional experts according to the particularities of each situation. It involves the use of local resources, as we mentioned earlier, and the implementation of a fundraising strategy. With a

Workshop discussion organized by the Union of Community Museums of Oaxaca, held in Caca-opera, El Salvador, July 2001. Photograph courtesy of Cuauhtémoc Camarena.

community museum, it is always a priority to develop local participation. In some cases, such as the indigenous communities of Oaxaca, the local population will contribute days of free communal labor to work on the building. In other communities, it is possible to invite the local population to volunteer in a variety of tasks, from creating a garden to installing a wooden panel.

The development of support networks with other museums, organizations, and communities is an effective strategy to gain access to a variety of training resources and to facilitate peer learning. The mutual support and solidarity generated in exchanges allow local communities to increase their motivation, optimism, and energy for their work. Exchanges also provide points of reference for each community to contrast and analyze their specific situations, while they clarify and enrich their vision of the museum.

The obstacles to be faced in these initial stages are many, but the most serious one is often the breakdown of traditional ways of resolving community conflicts; this breakdown often means that any initiative can be subject to attack from diverse factions and will not be able to gain significant support. Frequently the initiators of a community museum become so attached to the project that they narrow the possibilities of local participation to the point where supporters practically disappear, then they complain about apathy, which they themselves have promoted. When they assume responsibilities or intervene in decisions that belong to the community, supporting institutions are sometimes an obstacle in themselves.

The role of an external agent or institution in this process is that of a facilitator, focused on providing information and building local capacities through training and guidance. The first initiators and the museum committee or local association can benefit greatly from clarifying the concept of the community museum and learning participatory methods to involve community members. One of the most successful strategies is for committee members to visit community museums and to learn from direct experience what they are and how they operate.

The supporting institutions must avoid directing the initiative and displacing local leadership. They should always act as consultants, providing information and advice, but not intervening directly in decisions the community must make for itself or fulfilling positions of responsibility in the operation of the project. Community members must take full responsibility and strengthen their own capacities to move the project forward. The central challenge to starting a community museum is to develop a collective decision-making process to approve the project and to build widespread consensus on its importance and value. Each community will arrive at this consensus by a unique path. A well organized, determined community will be capable of defining and successfully carrying out strategies to resolve the scholarly, technical, and financial issues that will arise later. The museum will fulfill its purpose when it has cultivated the strong roots that will sustain it in the minds and hearts of the community members.

NOTES

1. The National Institute of Anthropology and History of Mexico (Instituto Nacional de Antropología e Historia) has supported the project since 1985 through its office in the state of Oaxaca. From 1987 to 2000, the Inter-American Foundation provided essential support to the Union of Community Museums of Oaxaca, A.C. (UMCO). At present, the Rockefeller Foundation is providing for the program of community workshops of UMCO's training center. Other supporting institutions include the Instituto Nacional Indigenista, the Dirección General de Culturas Populares, the U.S.–Mexico Fund for Culture, Traditions for Tomorrow, Partners of the Americas, the Arizona Commission on the Arts, Atlatl, and UNESCO.

2. From September 29 to October 5, 2000, UMCO organized a meeting called "Creating Bonds: Ex-

change between Community Museums of the Americas." Forty representatives of communities that have established or that are in the process of establishing community museums from the U.S., Mexico, Guatemala, El Salvador, Nicaragua, Costa Rica, Panama, Venezuela, Ecuador, and Bolivia participated. These representatives formed the coordinating committee of community museums of the Americas, and developed a project to continue international exchange and organize training events. The representation of UNESCO in Mexico provided support in 2001 to carry out a series of ten workshops, one in each participating country, to clarify the concepts of methods of the community museum and to strengthen the network.

3. René Rivard, "Opening up the Museum," Quebec City, 1984.

4. Cuauhtémoc Camarena, Teresa Morales, and Constantino Valeriano, *Pasos para crear un museo comunitario*, CONACULTA, Mexico, 1994; Cuauhtémoc Camarena and Teresa Morales, *Fortaleciendo lo propio: ideas para la creación de un museo communitario*, CONACULTA, Oaxaca, 1995.

5. Kevin Healy, *Llamas, Weavings, and Organic Chocolate*, South Bend, Indiana: University of Notre Dame Press, 2001; Alicia M. Barabas and Miguel A. Bartolomé, *Pluralidad en peligro*, INA–INI, Mexico, 1996; Enrique Leff, *Saber ambiental: sustentabilidad, racionalidad, complejidad, poder*, Siglo XXI Editores, México, 1998.

6. In Oaxaca, and other areas where indigenous cultures persist in Mexico, community members can generate consensus through the village assembly, which carries out the approval of the community museum project, the election of the museum committee, and the selection of themes and the building. In the central and northern states of Mexico, however, *asociaciones civiles* are more common, and community museums are organized by developing links to local schools, local cultural groups, and neighborhood associations.

7. *Pasos para crear*, pp. 37–39

8. Cuauhtémoc Camarena and Teresa Morales, *Communities Creating Exhibitions/Comunidades creando exposiciones*, Fideicomiso para la Cultura México/USA, Centro INAH Oaxaca, Oaxaca, 1999.

RESOURCES

Camarena, Cuauhtémoc, Teresa Morales, and Constantino Valeriano. *Pasos para crear un museo comuntario*. México: CONACULTA, 1994.

Camarena, Cuauhtémoc, and Teresa Morales. *Fortaleciendo lo propio: ideas para la creación de un museo comunitario*. México: CONACULTA, 1995.

Camarena, Cuauhtémoc, and Teresa Morales. *Communities Creating Exhibitions/Comunidades creando exposiciones*. Fideicomiso para la Cultura México/USA, Centro INAH Oaxaca, Oaxaca, México, 1999.

Fuller, Nancy. "The Museum as a Vehicle for Community Empowerment: The Ak-Chin Indian Community Ecomuseum Project." In *Museums and Communities*, edited by Ivan Karp et al. Washington and London: Smithsonian Institution Press, 1992.

Hauenschild, Andrea. "Claims and Reality of the New Museology." Ph.D. dissertation, University of Hamburg, 1988.

Morales, Teresa. "Cultural Appropriation in Community Museums." Bulletin, Center for Museum Studies, Smithsonian Institution, September 1996.

Rivard, René. "Opening up the Museum." Unpublished document. Quebec City, 1984.

Three Affiliated Tribes Museum director Marilyn Hudson (fourth from right) and museum staff remove plaques honoring Mandan, Arikara, and Hidatsa chiefs from the historic Four Bears Bridge and relocate them to the museum for safe-keeping. Photograph by Phyllis Cross.

MARILYN C. HUDSON

VOLUNTEERISM AND THE
THREE AFFILIATED TRIBES MUSEUM

The Three Affiliated Tribes, or the Mandan, Hidatsa, and Arikara, believe their existence in North America to date from the beginning of time. The tribes lived in villages along the Missouri River for centuries before coming into contact with Europeans, and they began formalizing their union in 1862.

The Three Affiliated Tribes Museum, located on the Fort Berthold Reservation in New Town, North Dakota, originated almost a half century ago after the discovery of oil in the Williston Basin in North Dakota. The discovery led to mineral rights for Helen Gough, an Arikara member of the Three Affiliated Tribes. Revenue from her several oil wells on and off the reservation helped build a heritage center for the Mandan, Hidatsa, and Arikara people and provide scholarships for Indian students. Gough did not live to see the Three Affiliated Tribes Museum open in 1964.

By the early 1950s, the waters of the Garrison Dam and Reservoir, built in the late 1940s, had flooded the Missouri Valley and displaced the Mandan, Hidatsa, and Arikara. The group was witnessing its history, culture, and communities deteriorating, if not disappearing. In the early 1960s, when Gough's modest heritage center was erected, the Fort Berthold people were still recovering from the trauma of displacement from the Missouri River bottomlands. Severe economic conditions meant that nearly all tribal resources had to be devoted to the daily needs of the people.

If Helen Gough planted the seed for a museum, that seed survived and flour-ished largely due to volunteer efforts. Although living in a socially and eco-nomically depressed area, the people of Fort Berthold Reservation gener-ously donated valuable items to the museum for its collection and devoted hours of service on the board of directors (several original board members still serve in that capacity). The economic conditions of the time constrained the operation and maintenance of the museum; for many years cash flow was too limited to do much more than keep the doors open.

Since then, the success of the museum has simply mirrored the positive forces outside its walls, such as the steady economic growth in the region and on the reservation, the renewed interest in tribal history, and the grow-ing numbers of elders. Also, activities like those planned for the 2002 Lewis and Clark Bicentennial, which included an exhibition at the Three Tribes Museum, drew interest to the area.

The Mandan, Hidatsa, and Arikara people have long been known for their generosity. It is the spirit of selflessness that ensures the survival of a people. In the tribal group, roles and responsibilities are well-defined through clanship and kinship ties. Many of the ancient traditions—such as ceremo-nials, harvest festivals, and trade fairs—are no longer practiced; however, through such "modern" pursuits as serving on boards and organizations such as the American Legion or belonging to tribal social clubs, tribal mem-bers make cultural contributions informed by a strong sense of tribal tra-dition and community service. About 5,000 tribal members now live on the Fort Berthold Reservation. Many of the museum's most successful projects have come about through strong community support and interest.

In 1993, the museum sponsored an Elbowoods School reunion, the first since the school closed in 1953 when the Garrison Dam was constructed. The flooding of the valley included the Indian community of Elbowoods, the site of which is under Lake Sakakawea. A committee made up of for-mer students organized the event. The community's response was overwhelm-ing: the reunion committee received photos, mementos, clothing, and arti-facts, as well as eight-millimeter film clips. These items led to a successful

Left: Marilyn Hudson standing next to a monument in honor of Four Bears, chief of the Mandans, dedicated in 1934. Photograph courtesy of the Three Affiliated Tribes Museum.

Below: A side view of the Three Affiliated Tribes Museum. Located on reservation lands of the Arikara, Hidatsa, and Mandan tribes, the building was originally a church. Photograph courtesy of the Three Affiliated Tribes Museum.

reunion and an excellent multimedia history of the Elbowoods School era that was later donated to the museum. The tribal government, researchers, and others interested in that period of the Three Affiliated Tribe's history refer to this collection of materials; the collection also played a relevant part in a hearing before a Senate Committee on Indian Affairs regarding the pre-Garrison Dam educational system.

In 1995, a World War II commemorative committee, consisting of family members of veterans, developed an exhibit depicting the men and women who served in the war. The community responded, wanting to be sure that the contributions of their family members were presented in the exhibit. The museum gained a valuable collection of photos, oral and written history, and memorabilia from that period, covering not only servicemen and -women, but those on the home front as well. This exhibit awakened the community's kinship ties and the tribal tradition of recognition and honor for those who served as warriors or in service to their country.

In 2000 a committee formed to commemorate the 150th anniversary of the Fort Laramie Treaty designed an exhibit. The 1851 treaty originally established the boundaries of the Fort Berthold Reservation for the Three Tribes at twelve million acres. Government allotment, however, would significantly reduce the acreage; the reservation now occupies half a million acres. The Fort Laramie Committee included descendants of the chiefs who took part in the Great Treaty Council—the delegation responsible for signing the document—as well as other tribal members who possessed the knowledge needed to plan the exhibition. The 2001 exhibit *They Touched the Pen: The Mandan, Hidatsa, and Arikara Treaty of Fort Laramie, September 17, 1851* featured the rededication of the Fort Laramie Treaty Monument, commemorations, and cultural fairs. Cleary, tribal members' cultural and familial ties to an historic event had spurred another volunteer effort with effective results.

The museum relies heavily on outside help for special projects. Potential volunteers all the more appreciate being asked to participate when they can bring their unique knowledge to benefit the tribe as a whole. People are especially willing to help out when there is a family or kinship connection to a project or exhibit.

Eastern Mennonite University President Dr. Joseph L. Lapp (right) accepts the gift of a quilt at a repatriation ceremony, March 15, 2002, in Harrisonburg, Virginia. Making the presentation are (from left) Marilyn Hudson, Edwin Benson (Mandan), and Daylon Spotted Bear (Mandan/Hidatsa). The quilt, sewn by Shirley Grady (Hidatsa), incorporates the university's colors and symbol. It was given by the tribe in gratitude for the university's repatriation of items including an eagle-feather headdress, a buckskin shirt with quillwork, beaded moccasins, beaded buckskin pants, and a war club. Photograph courtesy of Hannah Lapp.

The museum is also fortunate to have individuals assist in its daily operation, mainly retirees who are happy to contribute some free time to a project. And those who volunteer their knowledge and experience of reservation life before the construction of the Garrison Dam are invaluable to the museum and its visitors. Living links to the past, these elders are especially important to preserving their tribe's heritage. But young and old, Indian and non-Indian alike, many individuals volunteer their time. All people who have given their time to the Three Affiliated Tribes Museum are the guardians of the Mandan, Hidatsa, and Arikara, helping to fulfill the museum's mission.

Contributors

JANINE BOWECHOP (Makah) has served as executive director of the Makah Cultural and Research Center (MCRC), located in Washington State, since 1995. At MCRC, she also worked as a project researcher, then as curator of collections. She is chairperson of the Makah Tribe's Higher Education Committee, vice-chairperson of the National Association of Tribal Historic Preservation Officers, a board member of the Clallam County Historical Society and the Governor's Advisory Council for Historic Preservation, and vice-president of the Spirit Paddlers Canoe Club.

KAREN COODY COOPER (Cherokee Nation of Oklahoma) is the Museum Training Program coordinator for the Community Services Department of the Smithsonian Institution's National Museum of the American Indian in Washington, D.C. Included in the outreach programs she manages are the NMAI Internships, Visiting Native Museum Professionals, Museum Training Workshops, and Museum Technical Assistance/Consultation Programs.

RICHARD W. HILL SR. (Tuscarora) is a guest lecturer at the Six Nations Polytechnic in Ohsweken, Ontario, and the Tekarihwake Program in the Language Studies Department at Mohawk College in Hamilton, Ontario. From 1992 to 1995, Hill served as the assistant director for Public Programs and as the special assistant to the director of the National Museum of the American Indian. His essays and photographs on Native American life have been widely published.

MARILYN C. HUDSON (Mandan/Hidatsa) has volunteered at the Three Affiliated Tribes Museum for more than a decade, with an interest in researching the historically rich area of North Dakota. Hudson helped develop the following exhibitions and projects at the museum: *The History of the Elbowoods School, Early Ranching and Rodeo on the Fort Berthold Reservation, World War II and the Fort Berthold People, The Garrison Dam Era, The Four Bears Bridge, The 1851 Fort Laramie Treaty,* and *Indian Boarding Schools in 1924.*

MARILYN G. JONES (Suquamish) has served for ten years as the museum director for the Suquamish Tribe, located in Washington State. She enjoys traditional dancing, studying the Suquamish language, canoeing, walking, and reading. She believes visiting with elders and hearing about their life experiences is the best way to pass on culture and history to future generations.

JEFFREY E. MAUGER is a college instructor and former collections manager for the Makah Cultural and Research Center in Washington State.

CUAUHTÉMOC CAMARENA and TERESA MORALES coordinate a national training program for community museums in Oaxaca, Mexico, and act as consultants to the Union of Community Museums of Oaxaca, the National Union of Community Museums of Mexico, and the Coordinating Committee of Community Museums of the Americas. They began working with community museums in 1985.

NICOLASA I. SANDOVAL (Chumash) advises nonprofit organizations in cultural and educational resource management. She serves on the board of directors for the California Indian Museum and Cultural Center, the Santa Ynez Valley Historical Society, and the American Indian Advisory Committee for the Santa Barbara Museum of Natural History. She has dedicated her personal and professional life to increasing community access to artistic, cultural, and educational resources. Sandoval served as NMAI Assistant Director for Community Services from 1999 to 2002.

IRVINE J. SCALPLOCK (Blackfoot) is director of the Culture and Heritage Center at Siksika Nation, Alberta, Canada. His interests lay in repatriating all ceremonial material to the Siksika community and in initiating museum workshops and related cultural training. Scalplock travels extensively in Canada and the U.S., participating in cultural activities such as powwows, workshops, and ceremonies and serving as a consultant for ceremonial pieces and sacred objects.

SUSAN SECAKUKU (Hopi) has worked for her tribe on cultural preservation and tourism issues and with the Heard Museum in curatorial and collections. She worked with the Community Services Department of the National Museum of the American Indian for seven years, during which she developed and managed outreach opportunities for Native American tribes in museum training and operations. She has since returned to Arizona and is based on the Hopi reservation, where she serves as a contractor on tribal museum- and culture-related projects.

AMY F. STEFFIAN is deputy director of the Alutiiq Museum and Archaeological Repository in Kodiak, Alaska. An archaeologist who joined the museum at its inception, she designs public education programs on Alutiiq heritage. She is creator of the museum's *Alutiiq Word of the Week* and Community Archaeology programs.

Bibliography about and for Native Museums

Native Museums and Communities

Abrams, George H. J. "Tribal Museums in America." A report by the American Association for State and Local History, Nashville, TN, 2004. This document may be found on the AASLH website at www.aaslh.org.

Dyal, Susan. *Preserving Traditional Arts: A Toolkit for Native American Communities*. Presented by the American Indian Studies Center, University of California, Los Angeles, 1985.

Erikson, Patricia Pierce, with Helma Ward and Kirk Wachendorf. *Voices of a Thousand People: The Makah Cultural and Research Center*. Lincoln: University of Nebraska Press, 2002. An ethnographic study of a Native museum.

Guyette, Susan. *Planning for Balanced Development: A Guide for Native American and Rural Communities*. Santa Fe: Clear Light Publishers, 1996. Sponsored by the Pueblo of Pojoaque, describing the development of the Poeh Center.

The Changing Presentation of the American Indian: Museums and Native Cultures. National Museum of the American Indian and University of Washington Press, 2000.

Collections Information for Native Communities

Hoveman, Alice R. "Conservation Wise Guide." Rev. ed. by Scott Carrlee. Alaska State Museum, Juneau, AK, 2001. Can be downloaded from www.museums.state.ak.us.

Ogden, Sherelyn. *Caring for American Indian Objects: A Practical and Cultural Guide*. Minnesota Historical Society, 2004.

Exhibition Catalogs by Native Museums

Bell, Theresa Hayward, Stephen Cook, and Bob Halloran. *Gifts of the Forest: Native Traditions in Wood and Bark.* Mashantucket Pequot Museum and Research Center, Mashantucket, CT. 2000.

Crowell, Aron L., Amy F. Steffian, and Gordon L. Pullar, eds. *Looking Both Ways: Heritage and Identity of the Alutiiq People.* An exhibition publication project of the Arctic Studies Center, the National Museum of Natural History, and the Alutiiq Museum and Archaeological Repository. University of Alaska Press, 2001.

Doxtator, Deborah. *Fluffs and Feathers.* A resource guide accompanying the exhibit on symbols of Indianness, Woodland Cultural Centre, Brantford, Ontario, Canada, rev. ed., 1992.

Duncan, Barbara R. *Where It All Began: Cherokee Creation Stories in Art.* Museum of the Cherokee Indian, Cherokee, NC, 2001.

Hill, Dawn J. *As Snow Before the Summer Sun: An Exhibit on Our Relationship to the Natural Environment, A Resource Guide.* Woodland Cultural Centre, Brantford, Ontario, Canada, 1992.

Marchiando-Bracey, Patty, and George Williams. *Our Land, Our Culture, Our Story.* Indian Pueblo Cultural Center, Albuquerque, NM, 1997. Catalog of an exhibition presenting the story of the Pueblo people.

Slemmons, Rod. *The Eyes of Chief Seattle.* Exhibition catalog prepared by the Suquamish Museum, Suquamish, WA, 1985.

Tiger, Jerome. *Jerome Tiger: A Retrospective.* Cherokee National Museum, Tahlequah, OK, 1992.

Catalogs for Museum Information

AAM Bookstore. A catalog of museum publications. Visit www.aam-us.org.

AltaMira Press. A catalog of museum publications. For more information, visit the American Association for State and Local History online at www.aaslh.org or AltaMira Press at www.altamirapress.com.

KAREN COODY COOPER

DIRECTORY OF NORTH AMERICAN
NATIVE-MANAGED COMMUNITY MUSEUMS

The several goals for this directory include helping Native museums increase visitation, facilitating the networking that goes on among Native museums, and providing information about Native communities that care for object collections and create exhibitions. In fact, communities and individuals are responsible for a significant number of museums in North America. More than 200 Native museums exist in Canada, the United States, and Mexico, and more are being built every year. Some of these museums are large, well-designed, fully staffed operations with state-of-the-art exhibitions; some are small, tucked into rehabilitated facilities, relying on volunteer staff and using local talent to create displays from meager collections. The rest vary in size and accomplishment, just like museums in general.

To compile this directory, the NMAI Community Services Department developed a survey that allowed recipient museums to describe their institution and its relationship with Native people. The list of museums we surveyed was comprised of places found on our own mailing lists, in past American Indian museum directories, in general museum directories (listed under American Indian museums), by web searches, and from people in the museum field. Those receiving the survey could choose to note any of the following descriptors which might pertain to their institution:

- Located on tribal land
- Native owned or Native operated
- Board of directors, trustees, or controlling authority is majority Native
- Director/site manager is Native
- Majority of staff members are Native
- Founded by a Native group or individual

The resulting list of museums includes institutions that selected one or more of the descriptors and that have exhibited material available to the public.

For museums located in the United States, mailing addresses and information about the museum's physical location have been provided. In those cases where one address is listed and it is not labeled either "location" or "mailing address," those listings are one and the same. For the listing of museums in Mexico and Canada, the mailing address is provided. In all cases, if you are planning a visit to any of these institutions, we strongly suggest that you contact the museum to confirm their location and hours beforehand.

We have no doubt missed many institutions in this directory, and we apologize for those omissions. Corrections and additions may be provided to me by e-mail at cooperk@si.edu for posting on the NMAI website; an updated version of the directory may be found at www.AmericanIndian.si.edu.

UNITED STATES

ALASKA

Alaska Native Heritage Center
8800 Heritage Center Dr.
Anchorage, AK 99506
Phone: (907) 330-8000
Fax: (907) 330-8030
www.alaskanative.net
info@alaskanative.net

Aleut Museum of the Pribilofs
Location: 100 S. Church St.
Mailing address: P.O. Box 88
St. Paul Island, AK 99660
Phone: (907) 546-2312
Fax: (907) 546-2366
julies@tdxak.com

Alfred Starr Cultural Center
Nenana Native Council, City of Nenana
Location: 110 River Front St.
Mailing address: P.O. Box 70
Nenana, AK 99760
Phone: (907) 832-5520
Fax: (907) 832-5532

Alutiiq Museum and Archaeological
    Repository
215 Mission Rd., Ste. 101
Kodiak, AK 99615
Phone: (907) 486-7004
Fax: (907) 486-7048
www.alutiiqmuseum.com
receptionist@alutiiqmuseum.com

Chugach Museum and Institute of
    History and Art
Chugach Alaska Corp.
Location: 201 3rd Ave. and Washington St.
Seward, AK
Mailing address: 560 E. 34th St.
Anchorage, AK 99503-4196
Phone: (907) 563-8866 x151
Fax: (907) 563-8402
ChugachMuseum@chugach-ak.com

Ilanka Cultural Center
Native Village of Eyak
Location: 110 Nicholoff Way
Mailing address: P.O. Box 322

Cordova, AK 99574
Phone: (907) 424-7903
Fax: (907) 424-3018

Inupiat Heritage Center
North Slope Borough Planning Dept.
Location: 5421 North Star St.
Mailing address: P.O. Box 69
Barrow, AK 99723
Phone: (907) 852-0422
Fax: (907) 852-4224
www.north-slope.org/IHCsite/
beverly.hugo@north-slope.org

Kenaitze Indian Tribe K-Beq Interpretive Site
    at Chugash National Forest
Mailing address: P.O. Box 988
Kenai, AK 99611
Phone: (907) 283-3633
Fax: (907) 283-3052
www.kenaitze.org
slindgren@kenaitze.org

Museum of the Aleutians
Location: 314 Salmon Way
Mailing address: P.O. Box 648
Unalaska, AK 99685
Phone: (907) 581-5150
Fax: (907) 581-6682
www.aleutians.org
aleutians@arctic.net

Nay'dini'aa Na' Cultural Center
Location: Mi. 55.5, Glenn Hwy.
Mailing address: P.O. Box 1105
Chickaloon, AK 99674
Phone: (907) 745-0793
Fax: (907) 745-7154
www.chickaloon.org
cvschool@chickaloon.org

Simon Paneak Memorial Museum
North Slope Borough
Location: 341 Mekiana Rd.
Mailing address: P.O. Box 21085
Anaktuvuk Pass, AK 99721
Phone: (907) 661-3413
Fax: (907) 661-3414
www.north-slope.org/nsb/55.htm

Southeast Alaska Indian Cultural Center, Inc.
106 Metlakatla St., Ste. C
Sitka, AK 99835
Phone: (907) 747-8061
Fax: (907) 747-8189
www.nps.gov/sitk/
seaicc@gci.net

Yupiit Piciryarait Museum
Location: 420 State Hwy.
Mailing address: P.O. Box 219
Bethel, AK 99559
Phone: (907) 543-1819
Fax: (907) 543-1885
www.avcp.org/services/CulturalCenter.html
jhamilton@avcp.org

ARIZONA

Ak-Chin Him-Dak Eco-Museum
47685 N. Eco-Museum Rd.
Maricopa, AZ 85239
Phone: (520) 568-9480
Fax: (520) 568-9557
www.azcama.com/museums/akchin.htm

Arizona State Museum
University of Arizona
Mailing address: P.O. Box 210026
Tucson, AZ 85721-0026
Phone: (520) 621-6281
Fax: (520) 626 6761
www.statemuseum.arizona.edu

Canyon de Chelly National Monument
National Park Service
Mailing address: P.O. Box 588
Chinle, AZ 86503
Phone: (928) 674-5500
Fax: (928) 674-5507
www.nps.gov/cach/

Colorado River Indian Tribes Museum
Location: 2nd Ave. and Mohave Rd.
Mailing address: Rte. 1, P.O. Box 23-B
Parker, AZ 85344
Phone: (928) 669-9211 x1335
Fax: (928) 669-8262
www.itcaonline.com/tribes_colriver.html

Gila Indian Center
Gila River Arts and Crafts, Inc.
Location: I-10, exit 175
Mailing address: P.O. Box 457
Sacaton, AZ 85247
Phone: (480) 963-3981
Fax: (520) 315-3968
www.gilaindiancenter.com
gilaindianctr@gilanet.net

Hoo-hoogam Ki Museum
10005 E. Osborn Rd.
Scottsdale, AZ 85256
Phone: (480) 850-8190
Fax: (480) 850-8961
www.azcama.com/museums/
    hoohoogam.htm

Hopi Cultural Center Museum
Mailing address: P.O. Box 7
Second Mesa, AZ 86043
Phone: (928) 734-6650
Fax: (928) 734-7113
www.hopiculturalcenter.com
info@hopiculturalcenter.com

Huhugam Heritage Center
Gila River Community
Location: 4759 N. Maricopa Rd.
Mailing address: P.O. Box 5041
Chandler, AZ 85226
Phone: (520) 796-3500 x222
Fax: (520) 796-3501
www.griccrmp.com/Huhugam.htm

Kwapa Nawee U'as Kkusaaw Cocopah
    Museum
Cocopah Indian Tribe
County 15th and Ave. G
Somerton, AZ 85350
Phone: (928) 627-1992
Fax: (928) 627-2280
www.cocopah.com
museum@c212.com

Navajo Nation Museum
Navajo Arts and Crafts Enterprise
Location: Hwy. 264 and
    Post Office Loop Rd.
Mailing address: P.O. Box 1840
Window Rock, AZ 86515
Phone: (928) 871-7941

Fax: (928) 871-7942
www.wnmu.org/mcf/museums/nnm.html
gibrown@navajomuseum.org

Ned A. Hatathli Museum
Diné College
Mailing address: P.O. Box 37
Tsaile, AZ 86556
Phone: (928) 724-6654
Fax: (928) 724-3349
www.dinecollege.edu/cds/
    07_nedhatathli.html

Nohwike Bagowa Apache Cultural Center
and Museum
White Mountain Apache Tribe
Location: 127 Scout Rd.
Mailing address: P.O. Box 507
Fort Apache, AZ 85926
Phone: (928) 338-4625
Fax: (928) 338-1716
www.wmat.nsn.us/wmaculture.shtml

Quechan Tribal Museum
Quechan Tribe of Fort Yuma
Location: 350 Picacho Rd.
Mailing address: P.O. Box 1899
Yuma, AZ 85366
Phone: (760) 572-0661
Fax: (760) 572-2102

San Carlos Apache Cultural Center
Location: Hwy. 70, Mi. 272
Mailing address: P.O. Box 760
Peridot, AZ 85542
Phone: (928) 475-2894
Fax: (928) 475-2894

Tohono O'odham Nation Cultural Center
    and Museum
Natural Resources Department
Location: Rte. 19, Topawa Village
Mailing address: P.O. Box 837
Sells, AZ 85634
Phone: (520) 383-0210
Fax: (520) 383-2872

Yavapai Apache Cultural Center
Fort McDowell Indian Community
Mailing address: P.O. Box 1779
Fountain Hills, AZ 85268
Phone: (602) 837-5121

CALIFORNIA

Agua Caliente Cultural Museum
471 E. Tahquitz Way
Palm Springs, CA 92262
Phone: (760) 778-1079
Fax: (760) 322-7724
www.accmuseum.org
mhammond@accmuseum.org

Barona Cultural Center and Museum
Barona Indian Reservation
1095 Barona Rd.
Lakeside, CA 92040
Phone: (619) 443-7003 x2
Fax: (619) 443-0173
www.baronamuseum.org
info@baronamuseum.org

Cabazon Cultural Museum
Cabazon Band of Mission Indians
84-245 Indio Springs Pkwy.
Indio, CA 92203
Phone: (760) 238-5770
Fax: (760) 347-7880
www.cabazonindians-nsn.gov
jstapp@cabazonindians-nsn.gov

California State Indian Museum
California Parks Department
2618 K St.
Sacramento, CA 95816
Phone: (916) 324-0971
Fax: (916) 322-5231
hberry@ca.gov

Cham-Mix Poki (House of Our Culture)
Soboba Band of Luiseno Indians
Location: 23904 Soboba Rd.
Mailing address: P.O. Box 487
San Jacinto, CA 92581
Phone: (951) 654-2765
Fax: (951) 654-4198
www.soboba-nsn.gov
moyla@sobobo-nsn.gov

Cupa Cultural Center
Pala Band of Mission Indians
Location: 35008 Pala Temecula Rd.
Mailing address: P.O. Box 445
Pala, CA 92059
Phone: (760) 742-1590

Fax: (760) 742-4543
cupa@palatribe.com

Hoopa Tribal Museum and Historic Villages
Hoopa Valley Tribe
Mailing address: P.O. Box 1348
Hoopa, CA 95546
Phone: (530) 625-4110
Fax: (530) 625-1693
http://bss.sfsu.edu/calstudies/hupa/
    hoopa.htm
hvtmus@pcweb.net

Indian Museum and Nature Learning Center
Maidu Interpretive Center and Historic Site
1960 Johnson Ranch Dr.
Roseville, CA 95661
Phone: (916) 774-5934
Fax: (916) 772-6161
www.roseville.ca.us/indianmuseum
kbundgard@roseville.ca.us

Malki Museum
Morongo Indian Reservation
Location: 11-795 Fields Rd.
Mailing address: P.O. Box 578
Banning, CA 92220
Phone: (951) 849-7289
www.malkimuseum.org
malkimuseum@aol.com

Marin Museum of the American Indian
Location: 2200 Novato Blvd. (Miwok Park)
Mailing address: P.O. Box 864
Novato, CA 94948
Phone: (415) 897-4064
Fax: (415) 892-7804
www.marinindian.com
office@marinindian.com

Nuui Cunni Paiute Cultural Center
Location: 2600 Hwy. 155
Mailing address: P.O. Box 3984
Wofford Heights, CA 93285
Phone: (760) 549-0800
Fax: (760) 379-4350
nuuicunni@earthlink.net

The People's Center
Karuk Tribe of California
64236 Second Ave.
Happy Camp, CA 96039

Phone: (530) 493-1600 x.2202
Fax: (530) 493-2564
www.karuk.us
lcarpenter@karuk.us

Sherman Indian Museum
9010 Magnolia Ave.
Riverside, CA 92503
Phone: (951) 276-6719
Fax: (951) 276-6336
www.shermanindianmuseum.org
lsisquoc@charter.net

Sierra Mono Museum
Location: 33103 Rd. 275
Mailing address: P.O. Box 275
North Fork, CA 93643
Phone: (559) 877-2115
Fax: (559) 877-6515
www.sierramonomuseum.org
sierramono@sierramonomuseum.org

COLORADO

Southern Ute Cultural Center and Museum
Mailing address: P.O. Box 737
Ignacio, CO 81137
Phone: (970) 563-9583
Fax: (970) 563-4641
www.southernutemuseum.org
sum@frontier.net

Ute Indian Museum
Colorado Historical Society
17253 Chipeta Rd.
Montrose, CO 81401
Phone: (970) 249-3098
Fax: (970) 252-8741
www.coloradohistory.org

Ute Mountain Tribal Park
Ute Mountain Ute Tribe
Location: Hwy. 160 and 666
Mailing address: P.O. Box 109
Towaoc, CO 81334
Phone: (970) 565-9653
Fax: (970) 564-5317
www.utemountainute.com
utepark@fone.net

CONNECTICUT

Mashantucket Museum and Research Center
Location: 110 Pequot Trail
Mailing address: P.O. Box 3180
Mashantucket, CT 06338
Phone: (860) 396-6800
Fax: (860) 396-6850
www.pequotmuseum.org
Dholahan@mptn-nsn.gov

DELAWARE

Nanticoke Indian Museum
27073 John J. Williams Hwy.
Millsboro, DE 19966
Phone: (302) 945-7022
Fax: (302) 947-9411
www.nanticokeindians.org/museum.cfm
nanticoke@verizon.net

FLORIDA

Ah-Tah-Thi-Ki Museum at Big Cypress
Seminole Tribe of Florida
Big Cypress Seminole Reservation
Mailing address: HC 61, Box 21-A
Clewiston, FL 33440
Phone: (863) 902-1113
Fax: (863) 902-1117
www.seminoletribe.com/museum
museum@semtribe.com

Ah-Tah-Thi-Ki Museum at Okalee Village
Seminole Tribe of Florida
Hollywood Seminole Reservation
5710 Seminole Way, Suite S-2
Hollywood, FL 33314
Phone: (954) 797-5570
Fax: (954) 797-5579
www.seminoletribe.com/museum
museum@semtribe.com

Miccosukee Museum of Tribal and
    Natural History
Miccosukee Tribe of Indians of Florida
Location: Tamiami Trail and S.W. 8th St.
Mailing address: P.O. Box 440021
Tamiami Station
Miami, FL 33144

Phone: (305) 223-8380
Fax: (305) 223-1011
www.miccosukeeresort.com/museum.html

HAWAII

Kaua'i Museum
Kaua'i Museum Association, Ltd.
Location: 4428 Rice St.
Mailing address: P.O. Box 248
Lihue, HI 96766-1338
Phone: (808) 245-6931
Fax: (808) 245-6864
www.kauaimuseum.org
museum@kauaimuseum.org

IDAHO

Nez Perce National Historical Park
39063 U.S. Hwy. 95
Lapwai, ID 83540
Phone: (208) 843-2261
Fax: (208) 843-2001
www.nps.gov/nepe
NEPE_Visitor_Information@nps.gov

Shoshone-Bannock Tribal Museum
Mailing address: P.O. Box 306
Fort Hall, ID 83203
Phone: (208) 237-9791

ILLINOIS

Trickster Gallery
American Indian Center of Chicago
190 S. Roselle Rd.
Schaumburg, IL 60193
Phone: (847) 301-2090
Fax: (773) 275-5874
www.trickstergallery.org
aic50@aic-chicago.org

KANSAS

Native American Heritage Museum
Kansas State Historical Society Site
1737 Elgin Rd.
Highland, KS 66035

Phone: (785) 442-3304
www.kshs.org/places/nativeamerican
nahm@kshs.org

Tribal Museum of Sac and Fox Nation
Sac and Fox Nation of Missouri in
    Kansas and Nebraska
Location: 106 Main
Mailing address: 305 N. Main
Reserve, KS 66434
Phone: (785) 742-7471
Fax: (785) 742-3785
www.sacfoxnation.org/museum.html

LOUISIANA

Chitimacha Museum
Chitimacha Tribe of Louisiana
Location: 3289 Chitimacha Trail
Mailing address: P.O. Box 661
Charenton, LA 70523
Phone: (337) 923-4830
Fax: (337) 923-6848
www.chitimacha.com
kswalden@chitimacha.gov

Tunica-Biloxi Museum
Location: 171 Yuroni Trail
Mailing address: P.O. Box 1589
Marksville, LA 71351
Phone: (318) 253-8174
Fax: (318) 253-7711
www.tunica.org/museum.htm
museum@tunica.org

MAINE

Penobscot Nation Museum
Location: 5 Downstreet St.
Mailing address: 12 Wabanaki Way, Indian
Island
Old Town, ME 04468
Phone: (207) 827-4153
www.penobscotnation.org/museum/
firekpr@hotmail.com

Waponahki Museum and Resource Center
Pleasant Point Reservation
Mailing address: P.O. Box 343
Perry, ME 04667

Phone: (207) 853-4001
Fax: (207) 853-6039
www.wabanaki.com
dolly@wabanaki.com

MARYLAND

Accohannock Indian Museum
Location: 28380 Crisfield Marion Rd.
Mailing address: P.O. Box 404
Marion, MD 21838
Phone: (410) 623-2660
Fax: (410) 623-2079
www.skipjack.net/le_shore/accohannock/
    museum.html
accohannock@dmv.com

Piscataway Indian Museum
American Indian Cultural Center, Inc.
16816 Country Ln.
Waldorf, MD 20613
Phone: (301) 782-2224
Fax: (301) 782-2225
www.piscatawayindians.org
piscatawayindians@yahoo.com

MASSACHUSETTS

Mashpee Wampanoag Museum
Mashpee Wampanoag Tribal Council
Location: 414 Main St.
Mailing address: P.O. Box 1048
Mashpee, MA 02649
Phone: (508) 477-0208
Fax: (508) 477-1218
www.mashpeewampanoagtribe.com

Wampanoag Indigenous Program
Plimoth Plantation
Location: 137 Warren Ave.
Mailing address: P.O. Box 1620
Plymouth, MA 02360
Phone: (508) 746-1622 x8385
Fax: (508) 830-6026
www.plimoth.org
lcoombs@plimoth.org

MICHIGAN

Bay Mills Library and Heritage Center
Bay Mills Community College
12214 W. Lakeshore Dr.
Brimley, MI 49715
Phone: (906) 248-3354
Fax: (906) 248-2432
http://rpaserver.uproc.lib.mi.us/bmcc.htm
library@bmcc.edu

Ziibiwing Center of Anishinaabe Culture
    and Lifeways
Saginaw Chippewa Indian Tribe of Michigan
6650 E. Broadway
Mt. Pleasant, MI 48858
Phone: (989) 775-4750
Fax: (989) 775-4770
www.sagchip.org/ziibiwing
kdcronkite@sagchip.org

MINNESOTA

Bois Forte Heritage Center
Bois Forte Band of Chippewa
1500 Bois Forte Rd.
Tower, MN 55790
Phone: (218) 753-6017
Fax: (218) 753-6026
www.boisforte.com
rozeberens@yahoo.com

Fond du Lac Cultural Center and Museum
Fond du Lac Band of Lake Superior
Chippewa
1720 Big Lake Rd.
Cloquet, MN 55720
Phone: (218) 878-7582
Fax: (218) 879-4146
jeffsavage@fdlrez.com

Mille Lacs Indian Museum and Trading Post
Minnesota Historical Society
43411 Oodena Dr.
Onamia, MN 56359
Phone: (320) 532-3632
Fax: (320) 532-5625
www.mnhs.org/millelacs
millelacs@mnhs.org

Pipestone Indian Shrine Association
Pipestone National Monument
Mailing address: P.O. Box 727
Pipestone, MN 56164
Phone: (507) 825-5463
Fax: (507) 825-2903
www.authenticpipestone.com
customerservice@authenticpipestone.com

Red Lake Tribal Information Center,
    Archives, and Library
Tribal Council Headquarters
Mailing address: P.O. Box 297
Red Lake, MN 56671
Phone: (218) 679-3341
Fax: (218) 679-3378
www.redlakenation.org/history.html
rltibarc@mail.paulbunyan.net

Two Rivers Gallery
Minneapolis American Indian Center
1530 E. Franklin Ave.
Minneapolis, MN 55404
Phone: (612) 879-1780
Fax: (612) 879-1795
www.maicnet.org
info@maicnet.org

MISSISSIPPI

Choctaw Museum
Mississippi Band of Choctaw Indians
Location: Industrial Rd.
Mailing address: P.O. Box 6010
Choctaw, MS 39350
Phone: (601) 650-1687
Fax: (601) 656-6696
www.choctaw.org
mspencer@choctaw.org

MONTANA

Chief Plenty Coups State Park
Location: 1 Edgar Rd.
Mailing address: P.O. Box 100
Pryor, MT 59066
Phone: (406) 252-1289
Fax: (406) 252-6668
http://fwp.state.mt.us/lands/
    site_283264.aspx
plentycoups@plentycoups.org

Flathead Indian Museum
Location: I Museum Ln.
Mailing address: P.O. Box 46
Saint Ignatius, MT 59865
Phone: (406) 745-2951
Fax: (406) 745-2961

Fort Belknap Museum
Fort Belknap College
Location: U.S. Hwy. 2 and 66
Mailing address: P.O. Box 159
Harlem, MT 59526
Phone: (406) 353-2607
Fax: (406) 353-2898
www.fbcc.edu
schandler@mail.fbcc.edu

Ft. Peck Assiniboine and Sioux Cultural
    Center and Museum
Cultural Resources Department
Mailing address: P.O. Box 1027
Poplar, MT 59255
Phone: (406) 768-5155

Museum of the Plains Indian
Location: Hwy. 2 and 89 W.
Mailing address: P.O. Box 410
Browning, MT 59417
Phone: (406) 338-2230
Fax: (406) 338-7404
www.iacb.doi.gov/museums/
    museum_plains.html
mpi@3rivers.net

The People's Center
Confederated Salish and Kootenai Tribes
Location: 53253 Hwy. 93
Mailing address: P.O. Box 278
Pablo, MT 59855
Phone: (406) 675-0160
Fax: (406) 675-0260
www.peoplescenter.org
tours@peoplescenter.org

St. Labre Cheyenne Indian Museum
St. Labre Indian School and Educational
    Assoc.
Location: 1000 Tongue River Rd.
Mailing address: P.O. Box 216
Ashland, MT 59003
Phone: (406) 784-4511
Fax: (406) 784-6161
www.stlabre.org

NORTH CAROLINA

Frisco Native American Museum and
    Natural History Center
Location: 53536 Hwy. 12
Mailing address: P.O. Box 399
Frisco, NC 27936
Phone: (252) 995-4440
Fax: (252) 995-4030
www.nativeamericanmuseum.org
admin@nativeamericanmuseum.org

Museum of the Cherokee Indian
Location: 589 Tsali Blvd.
Mailing address: P.O. Box 1599
Cherokee, NC 28719
Phone: (828) 497-3481
Fax: (828) 497-4985
www.cherokeemuseum.org
infocwy@cherokeemuseum.org

Native American Resource Center
University of North Carolina at Pembroke
Location: I University Dr.
Mailing address: P.O. Box 1510
Pembroke, NC 28372
Phone: (910) 521-6282
nativemuseum@uncp.edu

NORTH DAKOTA

Three Affiliated Tribes Museum
Fort Berthold Indian Reservation
Location: 302 Frontage Rd.
Mailing address: P.O. Box 147
New Town, ND 58763
Phone: (701) 627-4477
Fax: (701) 627-3805
www.mhanation.com
tatmuseum@restel.net

NEBRASKA

Angel DeCorah Museum and Research
    Center
Little Priest Tribal College
Location: 601 E. College Dr.
Mailing address: P.O. Box 687
Winnebago, NE 68071
Phone: (402) 878-3313

Fax: (402) 878-2355
www.lptc.bia.edu
esmith@lptc.bia.edu

Ponca Tribal Museum
Location: 2543 Park Ave.
Mailing address: P.O. Box 288
Niobrara, NE 68760
Phone: (402) 857-3519
www.poncatribe-ne.org
shawneb@poncatribe-ne.org

NEVADA

Pyramid Lake Tribal Museum and Visitor
    Center
Pyramid Lake Paiute Tribe
Location: 709 State St.
Mailing address: P.O. Box 256
Nixon, NV 89424
Phone: (775) 574-1088
Fax: (775) 574-1090
http://plpt.nsn.us/museum/
plakemuseum@powernet.net

NEW MEXICO

A:Shiwi A:wan Museum and Heritage Center
Location: 02E Ojo Caliente Rd.
Mailing address: P.O. Box 1009
Zuni, NM 87327
Phone: (505) 782-4403
Fax: (505) 782-4503
www.aamhc_museum@yahoo.com

Indian Pueblo Cultural Center Museum
2401 12th St. N.W.
Albuquerque, NM 87104
Phone: (505) 843-7270
Fax: (505) 842-6959
www.indianpueblo.org
info@indianpueblo.org

Institute of American Indian Arts Museum
108 Cathedral Pl.
Santa Fe, NM 87501
Phone: (505) 983-8900
Fax: (505) 983-1222
www.iaia.edu
museum@iaia.edu

Jicarilla Apache Culture Center
Location: Hwy. 64 and Basket Ln.
Mailing address: P.O. Box 507
Dulce, NM 87528
Phone: (505) 759-1343
Fax: (505) 759-1342
www.jicarilla.net
jacc@jicarilla.net

Mescalero Cultural Center
Location: 169 Chiricahua Plaza
Mailing address: P.O. Box 227
Mescalero, NM 88340
Phone: (505) 464-9254
Fax: (505) 464-9191
bigrope@zianet.com

Poeh Center
Pueblo of Pojoaque
78 Cities of Gold Rd.
Santa Fe, NM 87506
Phone: (505) 455-3334
Fax: (505) 455-0174
www.poehcenter.com
georgerivera@poehcenter.com

Sky City Cultural Center and Haak'u
    Museum
Location: I-40 W., exit 102
Mailing address: P.O. Box 310
Acoma Pueblo, NM 87034
Phone: (800) 747-0181
Fax: (505) 552-7204
www.skycity.com
sccc@skycity.com

Walatowa Visitor Center and Jemez Pueblo
    Museum
Pueblo of Jemez
Location: 7413 Hwy. 4
Mailing address: P.O. Box 100
Jemez Pueblo, NM 87024
Phone: (505) 834-7235
Fax: (505) 834-2221
www.jemezpueblo.org

NEW YORK

Akwesasne Cultural Center, Library, and
    Museum
St. Regis Mohawk Reservation

321 State Rte. 37
Hogansburg, NY 13655
Phone: (518) 358-2461
Fax: (518) 358-2649
www.akwesasneculture.org
akwmuse@northnet.org

American Indian Community House Gallery
Location: 708 Broadway, 2nd Floor
Mailing address: 708 Broadway, 8th Floor
New York, NY 10003
Phone: (212) 598-0100 x240
Fax: (212) 598-4909
www.aich.org
ssense@aich.org

Ganondagan State Historic Site
Location: 1488 State Rte. 444
Mailing address: P.O. Box 239
Victor, NY 14564
Phone: (585) 924-5848
Fax: (585) 742-2353
www.ganondagan.org
friends@frontiernet.net

Seneca-Iroquois National Museum
814 Broad St.
Salamanca, NY 14779
Phone: (716) 945-1760
Fax: (716) 945-1383
www.senecamuseum.org
seniroqm@localnet.com

Shako:wi Cultural Center
Oneida Indian Nation of New York
5 Territory Rd.
Oneida, NY 13421
Phone: (315) 829-8801
Fax: (315) 829-8805
www.oneida-nation.net/shakowi
info@oneida.nation.org

Shinnecock Nation Cultural Center and
    Museum
Location: 100 Montauk Hwy. and
    W. Gate Rd.
Mailing address: P.O. Box 5059
Southampton, NY 11969-5059
Phone: (631) 287-4923
Fax: (631) 287-7153
www.shinnecock-museum.org
shinnecockmuseum@yahoo.com

Six Nations Indian Museum
1462 County Rte. 60
Onchiota, NY 12989
Phone: (518) 891-2299
redmaple@northnet.org

Tonawanda Reservation Historical Society
Mailing address: P.O. Box 516
Basom, NY 14013
Phone: (585) 343-9313 x34
trhs@goart.org

OHIO

Shawnee-Woodland Native American
    Museum
Shawnee United Remnant Band of Ohio
7092 State Rte. 540
Bellefontaine, OH 43311
Phone: (937) 592-9592
Fax: (937) 592-4458
makadasse@yahoo.com

OKLAHOMA

Ataloa Lodge Museum at Bacone College
2299 Old Bacone Rd.
Muskogee, OK 74403
Phone: (918) 781-7283
www.bacone.edu/ataloa
timothyj@bacone.edu

Caddo Tribal Heritage Museum
Caddo Nation
Location: Hwy. 152 and 281
Mailing address: P.O. Box 393
Binger, OK 73009
Phone: (405) 656-2344
www.CaddoNation-NSN.gov/Programs/
museum@caddonation-nsn.gov

Cherokee Heritage Center
Cherokee National Historical Society
Location: 21192 S. Keeler Dr.
Mailing address: P.O. Box 515
Tahlequah, OK 74464-0515
Phone: (918) 456-6007
Fax: (918) 456-6165
www.cherokeeheritage.org
info@cherokeeheritage.org

Chickasaw Nation Council House Museum
Chickasaw Tribe
209 N. Fisher
Tishomingo, OK 73460
Phone: (580) 371-3351
Fax: (580) 371-9769
www.chickasaw.net/heritage/250.htm
kelley.lunsford@chickasaw.net

Choctaw Nation Capitol Museum
Location: Council House Rd.
Mailing address: HC 64, P.O. Box 3270
Tuskahoma, OK 74574-9758
Phone: (918) 569-4465
Fax: (918) 569-4465

Citizen Potawatomi Nation Cultural
    Heritage Center
Citizen Potawatomi Nation
1899 S. Gordon Cooper Dr.
Shawnee, OK 74801
Phone: (405) 275-3121
Fax: (405) 878-5840
www.potawatomi.org
jfinch@potawatomi.org

Comanche Nation Tourism and Information
    Center
Location: 410 S.E. I-44 Unit-A
Mailing address: P.O. Box 908
Lawton, OK 73501
Phone: (580) 595-4941
Fax: (580) 595-4937
www.comanchenation.com/tourism.html
cnvc2003@sbcglobal.net

Comanche National Museum and Cultural
    Center
Mailing address: P.O. Box 6283
Lawton, OK 73506
Phone: (580) 492-4988
Fax: (580) 492-4017
www.comanchenation.com

Creek Council House Museum
106 W. 6th St.
Okmulgee, OK 74447
Phone: (918) 756-2324
Fax: (918) 758-1166
creekmuseum@sbcglobal.net

Delaware Nation Museum
Mailing address: P.O. Box 825
Anadarko, OK 73005
Phone: (405) 247-2448
Fax: (405) 247-9393
tfrancis@thedelawarenation-nsn.gov

Five Civilized Tribes Museum
1101 Honor Heights Dr.
Muskogee, OK 74401
Phone: (918) 683-1701
Fax: (918) 683-3070
www.fivetribes.org

Jacobson House Native Art Center
609 Chautauqua Ave.
Norman, OK 73069
Phone: (405) 366-1667
www.jacobsonhouse.com
jacobson@ahalenia.com

Kanza Museum
Kaw Nation
Location: 800 Grandview Dr.
Mailing address: Drawer 50
Kaw City, OK 74641
Phone: (580) 269-2552
Fax: (580) 269-1161
www.kawnation.com/Facilities/
    museum.html

Osage Tribal Museum
Osage Tribe
Location: 819 Grandview
Mailing address: P.O. Box 779
Pawhuska, OK 74056
Phone: (918) 287-5441
Fax: (918) 287-1060
www.osagetribe.com
kredcorn@osagetribe.org

Red Earth
2100 N.E. 52nd St.
Oklahoma City, OK 73111
Phone: (405) 427-5228
Fax: (405) 427-8079
www.redearth.org
info@redearth.org

Sequoyah's Cabin
Oklahoma Historical Society
Mailing address: Rte. 1 Box 141
Sallisaw, OK 74955
Phone: (918) 775-2413
Fax: (918) 775-2413
www.ok-history.mus.ok.us/mus-sites/
    masnum26.htm
seqcabin@ipa.net

Southern Plains Indian Museum
Indian Arts and Crafts Board
Location: 715 E. Central Blvd.
Mailing address: P.O. Box 749
Anadarko, OK 73005
Phone: (405) 247-6221
Fax: (405) 247-7593
www.iacb.doi.gov/museums/
    museum_s_plains.html
spim@netride.net

OREGON

Museum at Warm Springs
Mailing address: P.O. Box 909
Warm Springs, OR 97761
Phone: (541) 553-3331
Fax: (541) 553-3338
www.warmsprings.com/museum
maws@redmond-net.com

Tamástslikt Cultural Institute
Confederated Tribes of the Umatilla
    Reservation
72789 Hwy. 331
Pendleton, OR 97801
Phone: (541) 966-9748
Fax: (541) 966-9927
www.tamastslikt.com
info@tamastslikt.org

RHODE ISLAND

Tomaquag Indian Memorial Museum
390 Summit Rd.
Exeter, RI 02822
Phone: (401) 539-7213
Fax: (401) 491-9063
www.tomaquagmuseum.com
timm@tomaquagmuseum.com

SOUTH CAROLINA

Catawba Cultural Center
Catawba Cultural Preservation Project
Location: 1536 Tom Steven Rd.
Mailing address: P.O. Box 750
Rock Hill, SC 29731
Phone: (803) 328-2427
Fax: (803) 328-5791
www.ccppcrafts.com
wenonahh@ccppcrafts.com

SOUTH DAKOTA

Buechel Museum
Location: 350 S. Oak St.
Mailing address: P.O. Box 499
Saint Francis, SD 57572
Phone: (605) 747-2745
Fax: (605) 747-5057
museum@gwtc.net

Buffalo Interpretive Center
Lower Brule Sioux Tribe
187 Oyate Cir.
Lower Brule, SD 57548
Phone: (605) 223-2260
Fax: (605) 473-5465
www.lewisandclarktrail.com/section2/
    sdcities/pierre/buffalo.htm
lbst_tourism@yahoo.com

Great Plains Art Institute
Sinte Gleska University
Location: 381 E. 3rd St.
Mailing address: P.O. Box 8
Mission, SD 57555
Phone: (605) 856-8123
Fax: (605) 856-5401
www.sinte.edu

Harry V. Johnston, Jr., Lakota Cultural
    Center
Cheyenne River Sioux Reservation
Mailing address: P.O. Box 590
Eagle Butte, SD 57625
Phone: (605) 964-2542

The Heritage Center
Red Cloud Indian School
100 Mission Dr.

Pine Ridge, SD 57770
Phone: (605) 867-5491 x217
Fax: (605) 867-1291
www.redcloudschool.org/museum/
    museum.htm
heritagecenter@redcloudschool.org

Oglala Lakota College Historical Center
Pine Ridge Indian Reservation
Location: 490 Piya Wiconi Rd.
Mailing address: P.O. Box 490
Kyle, SD 57752
Phone: (605) 455-6000
Fax: (605) 455-2787
www.olc.edu

Sicangu Heritage Center
Sinte Gleska University
Antelope Lake Campus
Mailing address: P.O. Box 675
Mission, SD 57555
Phone: (605) 856-8211
Fax: (605) 856-5027
www.sinte.edu/heritage_cntr
heritagecenter@sinte.edu

TENNESSEE

Sequoyah Birthplace Museum
Eastern Bank of Cherokee
Location: 576 Hwy. 360
Mailing address: P.O. Box 69
Vonore, TN 37885
Phone: (423) 884-6246
Fax: (423) 884-2102
www.sequoyahmuseum.org
seqmus@tds.net

TEXAS

Ysleta Del Sur Pueblo Cultural Center
Tigua Indian Reservation
Location: 305 Yaya Ln.
Mailing address: 119 S. Old Pueblo Rd.
El Paso, TX 79907
Phone: (915) 859-7700
Fax: (915) 859-4252
tribalcouncil@elp.rr.com

VIRGINIA

Monacan Ancestral Museum
Monacan Indian Nation
2009 Kenmore Rd.
Amherst, VA 24521
Phone: (434) 946-5391 or 0389
Fax: (434) 946-0390
www.monacannation.com/museum.html
mnation538@aol.com

Pamunkey Indian Museum
Pamunkey Indian Reservation
456 Pocket Rd.
King William, VA 23086
Phone: (804) 843-4792
Fax: (804) 843-2504
http://home.earthlink.net/~pamunkey/
    museum.htm

WASHINGTON

Colville Tribal Museum
Location: 512 Mead Way
Mailing address: P.O. Box 233
Coulee Dame, WA 99116
Phone: (509) 633-0751
Fax: (509) 633-2320

Daybreak Star Art Gallery
Daybreak Star Indian Cultural Center
Discovery Park
Mailing address: P.O. Box 99100
Seattle, WA 98139
Phone: (206) 285-4425 x10
Fax: (206) 282-3640
www.unitedindians.com/sacredcircle.html
info@unitedindians.com

Lelooska Museum
Lelooska Foundation
Location: 165 Merwin Village Rd.
Mailing address: P.O. Box 526
Ariel, WA 98603
Phone: (360) 225-9522
Fax: (360) 225-7416
www.lelooska.org
lelooska_foundation@yahoo.com

Lummi Records, Archives, and
    Museum Collections
The Lummi Nation
2616 Kwina Rd.
Bellingham, WA 98226
Phone: (360) 384-2246
Fax: (360) 312-8742
juanj@lummi-nsn.gov

Makah Cultural and Research Center
Makah Nation
Location: 1880 Bayview Ave.
Mailing address: P.O. Box 160
Neah Bay, WA 98357
Phone: (360) 645-2711
Fax: (360) 645-2656
www.makah.com/mcrchome.htm
makahmuseum@centurytel.net

Quinault Cultural Center and Museum
Location: 807 5th Ave.
Mailing address: P.O. Box 189
Taholah, WA 98587
Phone: (360) 276-8211
Fax: (360) 276-4191
www.quinaultindiannation.com
ljones@quinault.org

Skokomish Tribal Center and Museum
N. 80 Tribal Center Rd.
Skokomish Nation, WA 98584
Phone: (360) 426-4232
Fax: (360) 877-5943
www.skokomish.org
dmiller@skokomish.org

Steilacoom Tribal Cultural Center
    and Museum
Location: 1515 Lafayette St.
Mailing address: P.O. Box 88419
Steilacoom, WA 98388
Phone: (253) 584-6308
Fax: (253) 584-0224
http://members.shaw.ca/nyjack/
    steilacoom/
steilacoomtribe@msn.com

Suquamish Museum
Suquamish Indian Tribe
Location: 15838 Sandy Hook Rd.
Mailing address: P.O. Box 498
Suquamish, WA 98392-0498
Phone: (360) 394-8496

Fax: (360) 598-6295
www.suquamish.nsn.us/museum
mjones@suquamish.nsn.us

Wanapum Heritage Center
Location: Wanapum Dam Hwy. 243
Mailing address: 15655 Wanapum Village
Ln. S.W.
Beverly, WA 99321
Phone: (509) 754-5088 x2571
Fax: (509) 766-2522
www.gcpud.org/culturalresources/
    wanapum.htm
abuck@gcpud.org

Yakama Nation Museum
Yakama Nation
Location: 100 Speel-yi Loop
Mailing address: P.O. Box 151
Toppenish, WA 98948
Phone: (509) 865-2800
Fax: (509) 865-5749
www.yakamamuseum.com

WISCONSIN

Arvid E. Miller Memorial Library
    and Museum
Stockbridge-Munsee Nation
Location: N 8510 Mohheconnuck Rd.
Mailing address: P.O. Box 70
Bowler, WI 54416
Phone: (715) 793-4270
Fax: (715) 793-4836
www.mohican-nsn.gov/TribalOffices/
    LibraryMuseum.htm
library.museum@mohican-nsn.gov

George W. Brown, Jr., Ojibwe Museum
    and Cultural Center
Location: 603 Peace Pipe Rd.
Mailing address: P.O. Box 804
Lac du Flambeau, WI 54538
Phone: (715) 588-3333
Fax: (715) 588-2355
www.lacduflambeauchamber.com
ldfpast@newnorth.net

Menominee Logging Camp Museum
Menominee Indian Tribe of Wisconsin
Historic Preservation Dept.
Mailing address: P.O. Box 910

Keshena, WI 54135
Phone: (715) 799-5258
www.menominee.nsn.gov
mah22@frontiernet.net

Oneida Nation Museum
Oneida Nation of Wisconsin
Location: W892 County Rd. EE, De Pere,
WI
Mailing address: P.O. Box 365
Oneida, WI 54155
Phone: (920) 869-2768
Fax: (920) 869-2959
http://museum.oneidanation.org
museum@oneidanation.org

Winnebago Indian Museum (temporarily
    closed)
Location: 3889 N. River Rd.
Wisconsin Dells, WI
Mailing address: 5243 S. 42nd Pl.
Phoenix, AZ 85040
Phone: (602) 402-1687

WYOMING

David T. Vernon Indian Arts Museum
Grand Teton National Park
Colten Bay
Mailing address: P.O. Drawer 170
Moose, WY 83012
Phone: (307) 739-3494
www.nps.gov/grte/
alice_hart@nps.gov

Rupert Weeks Traditional Center
Shoshone Tribe
Location: 90 Ethete Rd.
Mailing address: P.O. Box 1008
Fort Washakie, WY 82514-1008
Phone: (307) 332-9106
Fax: (307) 332-3055
www.wyshs.org/mus-shoshone.htm

CANADA

ALBERTA

Blackfoot Crossing Interpretive Center
Siksika First Nation
P.O. Box 1730
Siksika, AB T0J 3W0
CANADA
Phone: (403) 734-5315
Fax: (403) 734-5387

Native Cultural Arts Museum
Northern Lakes College
No. 1 Mission St.
Box 3000
Grouard, AB T0G 1C0
CANADA
Phone: (780) 751-3306
Fax: (780) 751-3308
www.northernlakescollege.ca
myrel@northernlakescollege.ca

Ninastako Cultural Centre
P.O. Box 232
Standoff, AB T0L 1Y0
CANADA
Phone: (403) 737-3774
Fax: (403) 737-3786
cgwells@telusplanet.net

Tsuu T'ina Museum
Box 135
3700 Anderson Rd. S.W.
Calgary, AB T2W 3C4
CANADA
Phone: (403) 238-2677
Fax: (403) 238-0873

BRITISH COLUMBIA

Doig River First Nation Cultural Centre
4356 Doig Rd.
Box 56
Rose Prairie, BC V0C 2H0
CANADA
Phone: (250) 827-3776
Fax: (250) 827-3778
wreade@doigriverfn.com

En'owkin Centre
Green Mountain Rd.
RR 2, Site 50, Comp. 8
Penticton, BC V2A 6J7
CANADA
Phone: (250) 493-7181
Fax: (250) 493-5302
www.enowkincentre.ca
enowkin@vip.net

'Ksan Historical Village and Museum
P.O. Box 326
Hazelton, BC V0J 1Y0
CANADA
Phone: 250-842-5544
Fax: (250) 842-6533
www.ksan.org
ksan@ksan.org

Nkmip Desert and Heritage Center
1000 Rancher Creek Rd.
Osoyoos. BC V0H 1V6
CANADA
Phone: (250) 498-7901
Fax: (250) 498-7912
www.nkmipdesert.com
nkmipdesert@oib.ca

Quw'utusn' Cultural and Conference Center
200 Cowichan Way
Duncan, BC V9L 6P4
CANADA
Phone: (250) 746-8119
Fax: (250) 746-4370
www.quwutsun.ca
askme@quwutsun

Secwepemc Museum and Native Heritage
    Park
355 Yellowhead Hwy.
Kamloops, BC V2H 1H1
CANADA
Phone: (250) 828-9801
Fax: (250) 372-1127
www.secwepemc.org/museum.html
museum@secwepemc.org

U'mista Cultural Centre and Museum
1 Front St.
Box 253
Alert Bay, BC V0N 1A0
CANADA

Phone: (250) 974-5403
Fax: (250) 974-5499
www.umista.org
info@umista.ca

Xá:ytem Longhouse Interpretive Centre
Sto:lo Heritage Trust Society
35087 Lougheed Hwy.
Mission, BC V2V 6T1
CANADA
Phone: (604) 820-9725
Fax: (604) 820-9735
www.xaytem.ca
info@xaytem.ca

MANITOBA

Manitoba Indian Cultural Education
    Centre, Inc.
119 Sutherland Ave.
Winnipeg, MB R2W 3C9
CANADA
Phone: (204) 942-0228
Fax: (204) 947-6564
micec@shawcable.com

Urban Shaman, Inc.
203-290 McDermot Ave.
Winnipeg, MB R3B 0T2
CANADA
Phone: (204) 942-2674
Fax: (204) 944-9577
www.urbanshaman.org
inquiries@urbanshaman.org

NEWFOUNDLAND
AND LABRADOR

Torngasok Cultural Centre
Labrador Inuit Association
P.O. Box 430
Nain, NL A0P 1L0
CANADA
Phone: (709) 922-2942
Fax: (709) 922-2931
www.nunatsiavut.com
torngasok@nunatsiavut.com

NORTHWEST TERRITORIES

Dene Cultural Institute
Hay River Reserve
Box 3054
Hay River, NT X0E 1G4
CANADA
Phone: (867) 874-8480
Fax: (867) 874-3867
www.deneculture.org
info@deneculture.org

ONTARIO

Chiefswood Museum National Historic Site
1037 Hwy. 54
P.O. Box 640
Ohsweken, ON N0A 1M0
CANADA
Phone: (519) 752-5005
Fax: (519) 752-9578
www.chiefswood.com
chiefs@execulink.com

Manido Chiman Algonkian Heritage Centre
Algonquins of Pikwakanagan First Nation
1674 Mishomis Inamo
Pikwakanagan
Golden Lake, ON K8H 2N8
CANADA
Phone: (613) 625-2823
Fax: (613) 625-2332
www.algonquinsofpikwakanagan.com
rosscommanda@hotmail.com

Ojibway and Cree Cultural Centre
Mattagami First Nation
273 Third Ave., Ste. 204
Timmins, ON P4N 1E2
CANADA
Phone: (705) 267-7911
Fax: (705) 267-4988
www.occc.ca
info@occc.ca

Ojibwe Cultural Foundation Museum
West Bay First Nation
#15 Hwy. 551
P.O. Box 278
M'Chigeeng First Nation, ON P0P 1G0
CANADA

Phone: (705) 377-4902
Fax: (705) 377-5460
www.theocf.ca
info@theocf.ca

Ronathahon:ni Cultural Centre
North American Indian Traveling College
#1 Ronathahonni Ln.
Akwesasne, ON K6H 5R7
CANADA
Phone: (613) 932-9452
Fax: (613) 932-0092
ronathahonni@bellnet.ca

Wikwemikong Interpretive/Heritage Centre
64-3 Beach Rd.
Wikwemikong, ON P0P 2J0
CANADA
Phone: (705) 859-2385
Fax: (705) 859-2980
www.wikwemikongheritage.org
dpeltier@wikwemikongheritage.org

Woodland Cultural Centre
184 Mohawk St.
P.O. Box 1506
Brantford, ON N3T 5V6
CANADA
Phone: (519) 759-2650
Fax: (519) 759-8912
www.woodland-centre.on.ca/
museum@woodland-centre.on.ca

QUEBEC

Kanien'kehaka Raotitiohkwa Cultural Center
Kahnaw:ke Mohawk Territory
P.O. Box 969
Kahnawake, QC J0L 1B0
CANADA
Phone: (450) 638-0880
Fax: (450) 638-0920
http://library.usask.ca/native/directory/
    english/kanienkehaka.html
krcc.kahnawake@sympatico.ca

Kitigan Zibi Anishinaabeg Cultural
    Education Centre
Kitigan Zibi Anishinaabeg First Nation
54 Makwa Mikan
41 Kikinamage Mikan

Maniwaki. QC J9E 3BI
CANADA
Phone: (819) 441-1655
Fax: (819) 441-2665
www.kza.qc.ca
sylvia.morin@kza.qc.ca

Maison Tsawenhohi
75, Nicolas Vincent
Wendake, QC G0A 4V0
CANADA
Phone: (418) 845-0700
Fax: (418) 845-0030
maisontsawenhohi@cnhw.qc.ca

Musee Des Abenakis
108 Waban-aki St.
Odanak, QC J0G IH0
CANADA
Phone: (450) 568-2600
Fax: (450) 568-5959
www.abenakis.ca/musee/index.html
info@museedeabenakis.ca

Musée amérindien de Mashteuiatsh
1787, rue Amishk
Mashteuitsh, QC G0W 2H0
CANADA
Phone: (418) 275-4842
Fax: (418) 275-7494
www.museeilnu.ca
museeilnu@cgocable.ca

Saputik Museum
Puvirntuq Nunavik, QC J0M IP0
CANADA
Phone: (819) 254-8919
Fax: (819) 254-8148
www.avataq.qc.ca
avataq@avataq.qc.ca

Daniel Weetaluktuk Museum
Avatuq Cultural Institute
General Delivery
Inukjuak (Nunavik), QC J0M IM0
CANADA
Phone: (819) 254-8919
Fax: (819) 254-8148
www.nunavik-tourism.com/
    inuitmuseum.html
avataq@avataq.qc.ca

SASKATCHEWAN

Saskatchewan Indian Cultural Centre
120 33rd St. E.
Saskatoon, SK S7K 0S2
CANADA
Phone: (306) 244-1146
Fax: (306) 665-6520
www.sicc.sk.ca
info@sicc.sk.ca

Wanuskewin Heritage Park
RR #4
Saskatoon, SK S7N 4T6
CANADA
Phone: (306) 931-6767
Fax: (306) 931-4522
www.wanuskewin.com
wanuskewin@wanuskewin.com

YUKON

Tage Cho Hudan Interpretive Centre
Box 135
Carmacks, YT Y0B IC0
CANADA
Phone: (867) 863-5830
Fax: (867) 863-5710
tagechohudan@northwestel.net

Teslin Tlingit Heritage Centre
Teslin Tlingit Council
Fox Point
Box 133
Teslin, YT Y0A IB0
CANADA
Phone: (867) 390-2526
Fax: (867) 390-2156
admin@ttc-teslin.com

MEXICO

BAJA CALIFORNIA

Museo Comunitario Comunidad Indígena
Cucapa El Mayor
Delegacion Carranza
Ejido Cucapa Indigenas
C.P. 21730
Mexicali, Baja California
MEXICO
Phone: (686) 5 43 76 17

CHIAPAS

Café Museo Café
Cabecera Municipal
C.P. 29220
San Cristóbal de Las Casas, Chiapas
MEXICO
Phone: (967) 6 78 78 76

Museo de Arte Hermila Dominguez de
    Castellanos
Avenida Dr. Belisario Dominguez Sur
    No. 51
Colonia Centro
C.P. 30000
Comitan de Dominguez, Chiapas
MEXICO
Phone: (963) 6 32 20 82

Museo Comunitario Chol-Tzeltal
Avenida Central, Barrio Chico, frente al
    parque
Ejido Petalcingo
C.P. 29915
Tila, Chiapas
MEXICO
Phone: (919) 6 71 20 01

Museo Comunitario Cuenca del Usumacinta
Domicilio Conocido
Frontera Corozal
Ososingo, Chiapas
MEXICO
Phone: (015) 2 01 59 57

Museo Comunitario Ji'tontik (Piedras
    Arenosas)

Abasolo Km. 58 Carretera San Cristóbal-
    Ocosingo
C.P. 29955
Ocosingo, Chiapas
MEXICO
Phone: (919) 6 70 79 91
Fax: (200) 1 23 84 25

Museo Comunitario Mkumkuy yis wiatzi
Domicilio Conocido
Colonia Centro
C.P. 29620
Copainala, Chiapas
MEXICO
Phone: (968) 6 11 01 74

Museo Comunitario Ñuu Kuiñi
Carretera Tlaxiaco - Putla
Rancho Santa María Cuqila
C.P. 69802
Tlaxiaco, Chiapas
MEXICO
Phone: (953) 5 54 07 16
cuquilamuseocomunitario@hotmail.com

Museo Comunitario Ora'ton
Calle Cementerio
Cabecera Municipal
29320
San Juan Chamula, Chiapas
MEXICO
Phone: (961) 6 80 40 00

Museo Comunitario Tos ngumguy
Cabecera Municipal de Tecpatan
C.P. 29620
Tecpatan, Chiapas
MEXICO
Phone: (968) 6 53 30 89

Museo Comunitario Vinikton
Avenida Central Poniente
Cabecera Municipal
C.P. 29710
Huitiupan, Chiapas
MEXICO
Phone: (555) 1 50 49 24

Museo Comunitario "Yuca Saa"
Plaza Cívica
Colonia Centro
Villa de Tututepec

C.P. 71800
Juquila, Chiapas
MEXICO
Phone: (954) 5 41 00 16
tututepec@hotmail.com

Museo de Cultura y Historia Natural Jave
    Pacuay
Primera Poniente y Segunda Norte No. 28
Cabecera Municipal
C.P. 29140
Ocozocoautla de Espinosa, Chiapas
MEXICO
Phone: (968) 6 88 00 44
Fax: (968) 6 88 00 48
www.raizindigena.org
clubtopos@yahoo.com

Museo de las Culturas Populares de Chiapas
Diego de Mazariegos No. 34
Barrio La Merced
Cabecera Municipal
C.P. 29220
San Cristóbal de Las Casas, Chiapas
MEXICO

Museo de Etnografico de Tecpatán
Carretera a Malpaso
Pueblo Raudales Mal Paso
C.P. 29600
Tecpatán, Chiapas
MEXICO

Museo del Mar
Isla San Marcos
Boca del Cielo
C.P. 30600
Tonala, Chiapas
MEXICO
Phone: (966) 6 64 85 11

Museo de la Medicina Maya
Avenida Salomón Gonzáles Blanco #10
Colonia Morelos
C.P. 29230 Apartado Postal 117
San Cristóbal de Las Casas, Chiapas
MEXICO
Phone: (967) 6 78 54 38
Fax: (967) 6 78 54 38
www.medicinamaya.org
omiech@prodigy.net.mx

Museo Municipal Sna jsotz'lebetik
Crescencio Rosas
Cabecera Municipal
C.P. 29350
Zinacantan, Chiapas
MEXICO

Museo Na Bolom
Avenida Vicente Guerrero No. 33
Barrio El Cerrillo
Cabecera Municipal
C.P. 29220
San Cristóbal de Las Casas, Chiapas
MEXICO
Phone: (967) 6 78 14 18
Fax: (967) 6 78 55 86
http://nabolom.org

Museo de Tradiciones
Barrio Santa Ana
Cabecera Municipal
C.P. 29150
Suchiapa, Chiapas
MEXICO

Museo ya tock hach winik
Domicilio conocido
Municipio Ocosingo
Naha, Chiapas
MEXICO
Phone: (015) 1 51 80 02

Museo Yash lum
Instalaciones de la Presidencia Municipal
Cabecera Municipal
C.P. 29930
Yajalon, Chiapas
MEXICO
Phone: (919) 6 74 01 19
Fax: (919) 6 74 00 93

Pok'o chu'ul bal
Norte entre 2 y 3
C.P. 30200
Venustiano Carranza, Chiapas
MEXICO
Phone: (968) 687 06 07

Yok Chij
Guadalupe Victoria No. 61
Cabecera Municipal
C.P. 29240

San Cristóbal de Las Casas, Chiapas
MEXICO
Phone: (967) 6 78 42 89

CHIHUAHUA

Museo Norawa
Antigua Escuela Secundaria
Colonia Guachochi
C.P. 33180
Guachochi, Chihuahua
MEXICO
Phone and Fax: (154) 3 00 02

Museo Towi
Domicilio Conocido
Colonia Rocheachi
C.P. 33181
Guachochi, Chihuahua
MEXICO

DISTRITO FEDERAL

Museo Regional Comunitario Cuitlahuac
Avenida Tlahuac-Chalco # 63
Barrio la Magdalena, C.P. 13070
Delegacion Tláhuac, DF
MEXICO
Phone: (55) 5 84 22 70
www.cuitlahuac.org
nahuatl@cuitlahuac.org

GUERRERO

Museo Comunitario Amuzgo de
    Xochistlahuaca
Domicilio Conocido, frente al Mercado
C.P. 41770
Xochistlahuaca, Guerrero
MEXICO
Phone: (741) 4 15 22 54
Fax: (741) 4 15 20 32

Museo Renacimiento Indígena
Plaza de las Tres Culturas
Colonia Centro
C.P. 41200
Huamuxtitlan, Guerrero
MEXICO

OAXACA

Museo Comunitario Balaa Xtee Guech Gulal
Plaza Cívica
Pueblo Teotitlán del Valle
C.P. 70420
Teotitlán del Valle, Oaxaca
MEXICO
Phone: (951) 5 24 41 23
www.inah.gob.mx

Museo Comunitario Monte Flor
Plaza Cívica
Cerro Marín
C.P. 68482
San Juan Bautista Valle Nacional, Oaxaca
MEXICO
Phone: (200) 1 23 05 89

Museo Comunitario Note Ujia (Siete Rios)
Plaza Cívica, frente a la Iglesia
Pueblo San Miguel del Progreso
C.P. 69803
Heroica Ciudad de Tlaxiaco, Oaxaca
MEXICO
Phone: (953) 5 56 46 35

Museo Comunitario Pijijiapan
Instalaciones de la Casa de la Cultura
Cabecera Municipal
C.P. 20540
Pijijiapan, Oaxaca
MEXICO
Phone: (918) 6 45 00 52

Museo Comunitario Shan-Dany
Plaza Cívica
Pueblo Santa Ana Del Valle
C.P. 70428
Santa Ana Del Valle, Oaxaca
MEXICO
Phone: (951) 5 62 00 70

Museo Comunitario Yu Kuni I
Conocido, San Jose Chichihual Tepec
Chazumba
C.P. 69000
Huajuapan de Leon, Oaxaca
MEXICO
Phone: (953) 5 40 91 31

Museo Comunitario Yucuhite
Plaza Cívica
Pueblo Santa Maria Yucuhiti
C.P. 71110
Santa Maria Yucuhiti, Oaxaca
MEXICO
Phone: (954) 5 53 41 40

QUERETARO

Museo Comunitario Ya Nfädi Yu Nohño
(Los Conocimientos de los Otomíes)
Avenida Juarez Agencia Municipal
Centro Ciudad Toliman
C.P. 76600
Toliman, Queretaro
MEXICO
Phone and Fax: (467) 3 19 95

YUCATÁN

Museo Comunitario Itzmal Kauil
Calle 31, esq. 28 al costado norte del
Convento Franciscano
Ciudad Izamal
C.P. 97540
Izamal, Yucatan
MEXICO
Phone and Fax: (995) 4 00 32

Museo Comunitario Kan Pepen
Iglesia de San Miguel
Pueblo Teabo
C.P. 97910
Teabo, Yucatan
MEXICO
Phone and fax: (997) 2 06 19

Museo Comunitario Peten Ak
Domicilio Conocido en Yaxche
Colonia Valladolid Centro
C.P. 97780
Valladolid, Yucatan
MEXICO

Museo Comunitario Ucajal Dziuil Chiich
Domicilio Conocido (a espaldas de la Iglesia)
C.P. 97945
Tahdziu, Yucatan
MEXICO
Phone and fax: (997) 4 40 50

Museo Comunitario Uyotoch Cah
(a espaldas del Ayuntamiento de Akil)
C.P. 97990
Akil, Yucatan
MEXICO

Acknowledgments

The National Museum of the American Indian and the Community Services Department offer their gratitude to the contributors featured in this book; they have thoughtfully recounted their impressions and experiences in starting tribal museums. The editors want to give special thanks to Teresa Morales for her invaluable help in identifying indigenous museums in Mexico.

We are grateful for the leadership, counsel, and support we received from NMAI Director W. Richard West, Jr. (Southern Cheyenne and member of the Cheyenne and Arapaho Tribes of Oklahoma), who is keenly aware of the trials—and immense satisfaction—that come with opening a museum with a distinctly Native focus.

The museum's Associate Director Tim Johnson (Mohawk) conceived of this book, and we are thankful for his vision. We also want to acknowledge the Smithsonian Women's Committee, which awarded a generous grant in support of the project at its inception. As the book developed, museum Associate Director Jim Pepper Henry (Kaw/Muscogee) provided content guidance and direction. Thanks also to others in the museum's Community Services Department, especially Amy Van Allen and Jill Norwood (Tolowa).

Sarah Plumer and Alyson Cluck lent their talents to help research the book's comprehensive directory. We also relied upon the considerable support Lynne Alstatt provided by finding and directing us to important resource materials.

Last but not least, Steve Bell created the book's attractive design, and Terence Winch, Tanya Thrasher (Cherokee Nation of Oklahoma), Amy Pickworth, Duncan Primeaux (Ponca/Osage), Kate Mitchell, and Christine Gordon provided key editorial guidance throughout the book's evolution.

—K.C.C. and N.I.S.